M. Dudley Rose's

Life Lessons from the Table

Recipes to Feed the Body,
Stories to Nourish Your Soul

Third Dimension Publishing titles may be purchased for business or promotional use or for special sales. For more information, please write to:
Book Sales, Third Dimension Group, Inc. PO Box 1845, Calhoun, GA 30703.

PRINTED IN THE UNITED STATES OF AMERICA

THIRD DIMENSION PUBLISHING and its logo, a number 3 enclosed in a box, are trademarks of Third Dimension Group, Inc.

To Publish Your Next Christian Book
Visit our website at www.thirddimensionbooks.com

First edition published 2007

Book design by Jeff Compton

Third Dimension Books
a imprint of
Third Dimension Publishing
PO Box 1845
Calhoun, GA 30703
www.thirddimensionpublishing.com

Third Dimension Books
A Imprint of Third Dimension Publishing
Atlanta

Art by
Mary Elizabeth Ingram
Director of Children's Ministries,
McDonough Presbyterian Church

Acknowledgements

The Session of McDonough Presbyterian Church in McDonough, Georgia, graciously granted me a mini-sabbatical leave to research and write this book.

▼ Laura Wigington (Mrs. Mike), Administrative Assistant at McDonough Presbyterian Church, proofread and typed the manuscript.

▼ Friends Jack and Kim North, Bobby and Jean Foster and Jane Foster, generously made available their "second homes" (Bonita Springs, Florida and St. Simons Island, Georgia) as beautiful surroundings in which I wrote the manuscript…as did the Koinonia Community in Americus, Georgia.

▼ The Norths, Elders at Second Presbyterian Church in Bloomington, Illinois, lovingly funded expenses I incurred during the mini-sabbatical.

▼ Additional financial resources required for the book's publication came as extraordinary gifts from Dee and Heather Anglyn, Derrell and Vicki Anglyn, John and Judy Davis, Rod and Betty Meadows, Lewis and Pat Robinson, Tommy Segers and Peter Thornton.

Disclaimer

Chefs know what they are doing…having a sense, whether by training or experience or both, that if this ingredient is paired with that one, a delightful taste results.

Cooks do not, without a recipe that chefs have imagined and created, know what they are doing.

I am a cook.

Table of Contents

Dedicated with Love

To Dorothy Ann Rose,

joy of my life,
and companion in cooking;

Frederick Buechner, speaking in 1997 at the installation of his
friend Douglass Hall as headmaster of Pennsylvania's
Mercersburg Academy, concluded,

*There are a lot of other things I could say about him,
but I'll limit myself to just one more, which is that his wife
is a winner in exactly these same ways and a good deal better
looking, so what you're really getting is two new friends for the
price of one. (SECRETS IN THE DARK – A LIFE IN SERMONS, 2006)*

Ditto Dorothy Ann.

February 4, 1988, the then Deland (Florida) Hilton and
Convention Center: I was standing near the "Please Wait
To Be Seated" sign at their restaurant for the "early bird special"
when a voice behind me asked, "Are you dining alone?"
Answering "Yes," the man said, "May I join you?" "Of course."
Fred Buechner and I, over prime rib ($17.33 for two, plus gratuity)
spent an hour talking…one of the most enjoyable and
helpful sixty minutes of my life.

With Appreciation

To Ed Albright, friend,
and cooking colleague.
A model for a host of us by valuing honor
more than fame, and friends more than success.

Glossary

"They," when not identified, refers to a
cooking class I've attended (Wolfe's Culinary
Center; Frank Copeland;David Glover;
Organic Market)... TV cooking channels
watched… *Articles in Bon Appetit, Cooking
Light, Food and Wine, Southern Living,
Gourmet.*

My favorite cookbooks:

River Road Recipes – The Textbook of
Louisiana Cuisine, 1959

A River Runs Backward – Flavors &
Reflections of Florida's First Coast, The
Junior League of Jacksonville, FL, 1995

James Beard's Menus for Entertaining, 1965

Glen-Ella Springs – Recipes and
Remembrances, Barrie Aycock, 1997

Cooking for the Weekend, Michael
McClaughlin, 1993

Stop and Smell the Rosemary – Recipes and
Traditions to Remember, Junior League of
Houston, TX; Three Rivers Cookbook I –
The Good Taste of Pittsburgh, Child Health
Association of Sewickley, PA, 1973

American Bistro, Diane Rossen
Worthington, 1997; Eat at Joe's – The Joe's
Stone Crab Restaurant Cookbook, Jo Ann
Bass and Richard Sax, 1993

Magnolia's Uptown / Down South Southern
Cuisine, Donald Barickman, 1995

HOSPITALITY
Genesis 18

Prayer: *Our Father, we thank Thee for those who have helped us along life's journey. For those who have cheered and inspired us and looked for the good in us that was often not immediately apparent, we give Thee hearty thanks. May we never withhold our help from those who are struggling and discouraged. As Thou hast blessed us so greatly, grant that we may continually strive to be a great blessing to our fellow men. In Jesus' name. Amen.*

(PRAYERS FOR ALL OCCASIONS, Stuart R. Oglesby, 1940)

Three men suddenly are standing at the entrance of Abraham's tent. It's high noon. The heat is suffocating. Father Abraham's immediate response is to offer the strangers his hospitality: water to wash their feet; the shade of a tree to sit under; orders to wife, Sarah, to prepare cakes using the best cornmeal in the kitchen; the tastiest calf in the herd to be roasted by the servants.

A Georgia building inspector suddenly appeared, just before noon, at the "Egg House" being refurbished by a crew from Koinonia Partners, Americus, GA…a house that will become a home for a low-income family. Jim, who directs such projects, wasn't on the site just then. The inspector insisted that the work be halted immediately because no certified electrician was present.

Standing in Koinonia's lunch line (fried and baked chicken, green beans, salad, salmon patties, rice, vegetarian casserole, celery soup, cornbread, blueberry cobbler, beverages) on that Friday in March, I overheard the young woman who had received the disturbing report from the building inspector explaining it all to Jim. I expected the veteran to lament the delay, etc. Instead, Jim's first statement was, "Did you invite him to lunch?"

Pecans are Koinonia's cash crop. Christian hospitality is their chief product. Would that our lives, and Christ's Church, mimic Koinonia more completely.

The eighteenth chapter of Genesis begins,

> The Lord appeared to Abraham by the oaks of Mamre…
> and behold, three men stood in front of him.

Readers of the story know right from the start what Abraham discovered only later: The three strangers speak for the Lord. St. Paul gives us a heads-up on the same truth:

Do not neglect to show hospitality to strangers, for thereby some have entertained angels unawares. (Hebrews 13:2)

Jesus drives home the truth with His astonishing assertion that when we feed and welcome the stranger, we're feeding and welcoming Him. (Matthew 25:37-40)

It couldn't be any clearer. God collecting a covenant people began with a noontime meal as Sarah and Abraham hosted the Lord by extending hospitality to three strangers. Jesus insists that when He returns to conclude history, the chief criterion of judgment ("sheep and goats" separated) will be whether we welcomed, fed and visited Jesus present in the stranger.

Hospitality…a mark of a Christian.

Ponderable

Koinonia Farm is an intentional Christian community located in the red clay farmlands of Georgia. To this community of believers, following the teachings of Jesus means treating neighbors equally, loving our enemies as well as our friends, and living a simple, shared life. Established in 1942, Koinonia's very presence challenged materialism, militarism and racism. In the 1950's the community endured bullets, bombs, and a boycott, but survived. Koinonia went on to give birth to many outstanding organizations, most notably Habitat for Humanity International. Today Koinonia remains committed to living in community, providing hospitality to visitors, and working for social justice around the globe. (229) 924-0391 www.koinoniapartners.org

AROMA

Thanks be to God, who in Christ always leads us in triumph, and through us spreads the fragrance of the knowledge of Him everywhere. For we are the aroma of Christ to God among those who are being saved and those who are perishing….

(II Corinthians 2:14-15)

Prayer: *Merciful God, we praise You that You give strength in every weakness, forgiveness for our failures, and new beginnings in Jesus Christ. Especially we thank You for the guidance of Your Spirit through this day; signs of new life and hope; people who have helped us; those who struggle for justice; and expressions of love unexpected or undeserved. Amen. (DAILY PRAYER, SUPPLEMENTAL LITURGICAL RESOURCE 5, Presbyterian Church, USA)*

We had no script. "We'll wing it," David said. He had prepared the ingredients for the three stews we'd make. The camera from Southern Crescent Broadcasting began taping the half-hour show,

"Hello, welcome to NOW YOU'RE COOKING. I'm David, chef and owner here at Truman's,
and this is my buddy, Dudley, Minister of McDonough Presbyterian Church. On
today's show we're going to demonstrate how to make stews. The first is a recipe for
curried lamb stew Dudley put together after spending a week in Jordan a few months ago….

and on we went. It was great fun. I'm grateful to David for the opportunity. We pulled the unrehearsed cooking show off quite nicely, thank you!

During one segment David and I found ourselves saying, almost at the same time, "It's a shame our audience can't smell the aroma of this food cooking. It's so delightful." We bantered on for another moment about not only how food is presented ("The eye tastes before the palate does") that makes a difference, but how the aroma / fragrance of most foods adds measurably to a diner's enjoyment.

Later I thought about a December, 2005, article I read by Kim Norris in the Detroit Free Press. She wrote that about 90% of taste comes from smell. Who would have guessed? In the unlikely event you're interested and don't already know: anosmia is the term for having lost the ability to smell… parosmia, distorted sense of smell… phantosmia, smelling aromas that aren't present (like the times I was sure that I smelled again the emission from the small Evinrude motor on the boat my dad and I took fishing most August mornings during my teenage years while vacationing on Torch Lake, Michigan)… hypernosmia, heightened sensitivity to scents. (I suspect wine sniffers and tasters lead this group)

According to the article, researchers at the Monell Chemical Sense Center in Philadelphia (our nation's only institution devoted to the study of the senses of smell and taste), estimate that 14 million Americans have one degree or another of "olfactory dysfunction."

About 90% of taste comes from smell.

About 90% of our Christian witness comes from the aroma of our lives,

…through us God in Christ spreads the fragrance
of knowledge about Him everywhere…

Some of us are stinking up the place. A reporter asked Ghandi what he thought about Jesus. "The greatest man who ever lived," he replied. "Then why aren't you a Christian?" "Because of the Christians I've met," he reported with sadness.

Then there is the sweet, attracting, compelling aroma of believers in league with Albert Schweitzer. Local dignitaries were present at Chicago's train station to welcome him, but he passed by them unrecognized because he was carrying two heavy suitcases for an older woman he'd met on the train who hadn't been able to find a porter. Eventually a reporter spotted Dr. Schweitzer struggling with the suitcases. "That's the first time I ever saw a sermon walking", he told his cameraman.

Let us go forth and classify ourselves.

Ponderable

I think what people really mean when they say they are against organized religion is that they're against hypocritical religion, misguided religion, blind or unthinking religion, religion of rules and laws rather than love, religion that comes diced and preprocessed and shrink-wrapped like ground beef. And that's what I'm against, whether it's in Hindu garb or Buddhist or Christian – especially Christian!
(Neo, in Brian D. McLaren's A NEW KIND OF CHRISTIAN, 2001)

SIMPLE
I Corinthians 1:18-23

Prayer: *Show us, O God, as much of Thy purpose as shall steady us. We do not ask that the way be made smooth, or even that Thou wouldst bestow upon us now the strength which Thou hast promised. We ask only for the grace to use what Thou has provided in Christ Jesus. Amen. (Paul Scherer, LOVE IS A SPENDTHRIFT, 1961)*

She died at age 89 in Decatur, Georgia, on a February day in the year of our Lord, 2006. South of the Mason-Dixon line, collectors of cookbooks prize her 1976 The Taste of Country Cooking, knowing it helped revive Southern Cuisine. Edna Lewis, author and chef who grew up on a farm, was one of the first African-American women to reach the pinnacle of the cooking world. According to Time,

> "She influenced chefs around the country with her insistence
> on simple recipes with pure ingredients."

He arrived at the Organic Produce Market in Atlanta's Virginia Highlands May 29th, 2004, on a fancy motorcycle with his eleven-year-old son tucked in behind him. About forty of us crowded around the small table where Chef Bruno Menard would demonstrate the techniques of making chilled tomato soup with lovage and fava bean pesto, complete with marinated watermelon and croutons.

Imagine the excitement: a bunch of amateur cooks up close and personal with one of America's premier chefs! His Ritz-Carlton dining room in Buckhead earned Mobil's Five-Star and AAA's Five- Diamond Awards for 2004. We embarrassed ourselves jostling for his autograph after the twenty- minute cooking demonstration, the only one Chef Menard does – that's how highly he prizes the Market's produce.

Extremely likable. Delightful sense of humor. Approachable. Nothing condescending as he answered our silly questions. You'll pardon me, but I thought of a couple "five-star clergymen" I've met who would do well to model themselves after this French-born culinary star.

The Chef made this observation,

> "If a recipe you're considering is too complicated, ignore it. The basics of
> good food are to always use the finest products and to keep it simple."

Riding back to McDonough that Saturday I thought about how, at this juncture in my faith journey, my experience of Christ has come to rest on "the simple basics." After years of academic pursuits, earning degrees, along with participation in countless continuing education seminars, lectures and courses, as well as shelves full of well-marked theology books, it's "the simple basics" on which I depend most:

- Jesus loves me, this I know, for the Bible tells me so….
- Amazing grace, how sweet the sound….
- Standing on the promises, leaning on the everlasting arms.

The same Market, September of 2005: different chef, same litany. You should have tasted the shrimp gumbo Scott Crawford of Food 101 created, beginning with a brown roux, then using the Market's produce (okra, shallots, four varieties of tomatoes and arugula)!

It took me longer than it should have to figure out why Chef Crawford named his Sandy Springs (North Atlanta) restaurant Food 101. During the cooking demonstration he kept saying things like,

> In your cooking, stick with the basics….depend on the tried and true…let others
> experiment with all the wild new combinations of tastes….People leave my restaurant
> saying "Your meatloaf was better than my mom's!"…Depend on the food and wines
> that you know from experience marry well.

The "simple basics;" Food 101; the introductory level course; the essentials that must be mastered before we can enroll in upper level classes and to which we often do well to return.

The Apostle Paul knew his "stuff." After all, he had the best theological education available (see Acts 5:34 and 22:3) at the feet of Gamaliel. But like Edna, Bruno and Scott, Paul knew "simple basics" were the key:

> (Others) seek signs and wisdom; we preach Christ, crucified.

Ponderable

There's a huge difference between a simple and a simplistic Christian faith…
between a childlike and a childish commitment to Christ.

SHARING
John 21

Prayer: *O God, You have set before us a great hope that Your Kingdom will come on earth, and have taught us to pray for its coming: make us ready to thank You for the signs of its dawning, and to pray and work for the perfect day when Your will shall be done on earth as it is in heaven. In the name of Jesus Christ. Amen. (IONA ABBEY WORSHIP BOOK, Scotland's Iona Community, 2001)*

Morning coffee is essential. Black and strong. Spare no cost. Dorothy's 2005 Christmas gift to me was a coffee bean roaster. I now turn green beans into perfectly toasted ones before grinding. For my taste, exactly twenty-three minutes per batch.

I recommend Café Campesino, Americus, Georgia (888-532-4728; www.cafecampesino.com), because they are a Fair Trade group founded in 1988 by Bill Harris, after what he labels "an enlightening experience with a coffee-growing family in Guatemala." The Café delivers organically grown "coffee with a conscience," roasted daily in small batches. The commitment to fair trade eliminates all the "middlemen," ensuring more profits for farmers all over the world. Please consider joining me in brewing their very special coffee. I'm delighted that we use, and sell, at McDonough Presbyterian, another Fair Trade coffee: Equal Exchange (www.equalexchange.com).

Ever since my year at Baton Rouge's Broadmoor Presbyterian as the Interim Minister, I've been a fan of their city's family-owned-for-85-years Community Club coffee ("the preferred retail coffee brand of New Orleans").

Vincent Van Gogh, son of a minister and an extraordinary artist, took his life in Room 5 of the French Inn, Auberge Ravoux, in a small village twenty-two miles northwest of Paris on July 29, 1890. A couple of years previously, he wrote his brother, Theo,

> "I spend most of my money on models. In the evening
> for supper, a cup of coffee and some bread."

In another letter to his sister, Wilhelmina,

> "For lack of money, I have been living from Thursday
> to Monday on 23 cups of coffee with bread."
> (VAN GOGH'S TABLE AT THE AUBERGE RAVOUX, Alexandra Leaf and Fred Leeman)

At least the "starving artist" had coffee!

My worst cups of coffee were endured in Jordan's hotels and rest stops. Inexplicably, they offer hot water over instant Sanka. My best cup of coffee was enjoyed at 11:35 a.m. on August 15, 2004, at the Silver Spoons Café in Naples, Florida, accompanying a club sandwich. I had "suffered" through two dreadful days without caffeine while spending a week reading and writing at Jack and Kim's winter residence in nearby Bonita Springs. Hurricane Charley had come ashore two days earlier. No electricity. I ventured out, knowing their car's air conditioner would provide welcome relief from the 100° heat index, hoping to finally get a cup of coffee and a bite to eat. The half-hour ride South on U.S. 41 (carefully, with power lines down and no traffic signals operating) brought the gift of Silver Spoons, open because of their own generator.

There is no mention of Jesus offering coffee to the seven tired, wet, frustrated fishermen that morning as the Resurrected One invited His disciples to be breakfast guests on shore at daybreak. I suspect a mug would have tasted as superb to them as did mine late on that August morning. But the Master did have fish frying and bread baking for His friends. Rather nice, don't you think, for those of us who enjoy preparing food, to ponder God's Son cooking.

If breakfast is ready, why does the Christ tell the fishermen, "Bring some of the fish you have just caught?" Lee Hastings Bristol, Jr., suggests,

> "Jesus was in the habit of giving those around Him a chance to make their offering to what He was doing, however small. We watched that happen when He accepted two fish and five barley loaves from a young boy's picnic basket. We see it now when He asks friends for some of their catch. When Jesus asked those tired friends of His for some of their fish, maybe He needed the fish and maybe He did not. Some theologians tell us maybe Jesus was merely encouraging them by letting them feel they were helping more than they were – like a mother who lets her young child feel she or he is helping her prepare dinner when the child really cannot do very much."
> (THE BIG PICNIC AND OTHER MEALS IN THE NEW TESTAMENT)

We're prone to call it "potluck" or "pitch in." Bring your contribution, small or large, homemade or store bought. Somehow, always, there is enough for all.

Sharing, a mark of the Christian.

Ponderable

"I'll pray that you grow up a brave man in a brave country. I will pray you find a way to be useful."
Gilead, Marilynne Robinson, 2004

LITERALLY
I Corinthians 11:23-26

Table Grace:

God of grace, sustain our bodies with this food; our hearts with true friendship; and our souls with Your Truth; for Christ's sake, Amen. (DAILY PRAYER – SUPPLEMENTAL LITURGICAL RESOURCE 5, Presbyterian Church, USA)

The instructions on the package of frozen peas were clear: Cook in one cup boiling salt water. When my mother returned home and asked why I hadn't started the peas for dinner, I explained the obvious: there was no way those peas could fit into a single cup of water!

I was a senior at Strong Vincent High School in Erie, Pennsylvania. One would think an eighteen year old could figure out the cup of water was first to be poured into a pot and then brought to the boiling point. Literalism can make fools of us.

When God's Son, in what we now call the words of the Sacrament's institution, said,

"This bread is My body; the wine My blood"

I doubt the Twelve took Him literally. They knew it was still a piece of flat bread; still vino fermented from local grapes. No magic words, even Jesus', transform whole wheat into divine flesh, Mogan David into literal human blood. Only a fool would obey, literally, Matthew 18:7-9:

Jesus said, "Woe to the world for temptations to sin! For it is necessary that temptations come, but woe to the man by whom temptation comes! And if your hand or your foot causes you to sin, cut it off and throw it away; it is better for you to enter life maimed or lame than with two hands or two feet to be thrown into the eternal fire. And if your eye causes you to sin, pluck it out and throw it away; it is better for you to enter life with one eye than with two eyes to be thrown into the hell of fire."

The psalmist's (96th and 98th) exuberant exaggerations, "…all the trees and the hills sing for joy before the Lord…the waters clap their hands!" are not true literally, either.

9

True, mind you. But Divine truth is more than, better than, literal…if we're "fools for the sake of Christ" (I Corinthians 4:10) and not just fools. One of many possible illustrations: Jonah surviving three days in the belly of a great fish. Literally? Not likely. But fools miss True Truth, Divine Truth, if we read the book of Jonah only literally…if we fixate on a literal interpretation of cook in one cup boiling salt water.

True Truth (I think that's Francis Shaffer's concoction) about Jonah is that he was a man who ran away from God instead of walking with God and thereby ran into a heap of trouble. The Divine One's marching orders were for the Jewish preacher to make his way by ship to Nineveh (Assyria) with the sermon that the God of Israel also loved the Ninevites. He booked passage, instead, on a boat bound for Tarshish – exactly the opposite direction from Nineveh. How could it be, an angry and spiritually arrogant Jonah demanded to know, that the God who he assumed was solely the possession of the Israelites, could possibly want to be Lord of an enemy population too?

To get the rebellious Jonah's attention, there ensues a storm at sea…Jonah's confession to the crew and passengers that he is the problem…his being offered as a "sacrifice" by being tossed overboard (walking the plank, if you will)…calmed waters…and a "great fish" (the story does not say "whale") to gulp him up for three 24-hour periods. Now Jonah is prepared to run to and with God, belatedly, obeying the original command.

What he feared happens: The people of Nineveh are converted. One imagines Jonah lamenting, wistfully, in Jonathan Swift's words,

> We are God's chosen few; all others will be damned.
> There is no place in heaven for you; we can't have heaven crammed.

Quite surprisingly, the story concludes with Jonah so sad over God getting His way that he wants to escape the unfortunate result by dying! Persistent (give him credit, I suppose) to the end, the preacher's protest has the reluctant messenger stalking to a shade tree and waiting for God to come around to his way of thinking.

God is still waiting for some of us to come around to God's way of loving. The bumper sticker could have been created with Jonah in mind: "God Loves/Blesses Everyone. No Exceptions."

Literally true: "This is My body/blood"? No. True Truth: "Do this in remembrance of Me" – to remember I love you; to remember my commandment; Love one another. Absolutely.

Ponderable

The Lord's Supper is make-believe. You make believe that the one who breaks the bread and blesses the wine is not the plump parson who smells of Williams' Aqua Velva but Jesus of Nazareth. You make believe that the tasteless wafer and cheap port are His flesh and blood. You make believe that by swallowing them you are swallowing His life into your life and that there is nothing in earth or heaven more important for you to do than this. It is a game you play because He said to play it. "Do this in remembrance of Me." Do this. Play that it makes a difference. Play that it makes sense. If it seems a childish thing to do, do it in remembrance that you are a child.

Remember Max Beerhohm's Happy Hypocrite, the wicked man who wore the mask of a saint to woo and win the saintly girl he loved. Years later when a castoff girlfriend discovered the ruse, she challenged him to take off the mask in front of his beloved and show his face for the sorry thing it was. He did what he was told only to discover that underneath the saint's mask, his face had become the face of a saint.
(WISHFUL THINKING: A THEOLOGICAL ABC, Frederick Buechner, 1973)

Entree

Cajun Sausage and Chicken Jambalaya

1 whole chicken
1 bunch green onions, chopped
1 lb andouille sausage, cooked and sliced
2 cups uncooked rice
4 chicken bouillon cubes
1 Tbsp. thyme
6 stalks celery, chopped
1 Tbsp. basil
1 large onion, chopped
1 Tbsp. (or to taste) Tony Chachere's
1 green pepper, chopped
Creole Seasoning

Boil the whole chicken in a stock pot full of water, 4 bouillon cubes and 3 stalks of celery. The liquid will produce your chicken stock, so save it. Cook chicken until very tender. Set aside to cool.

In a large skillet sauté 3 stalks of celery, 1 large onion and 1 green pepper. Cook vegetables until wilted, and then add green onions. When you have mixed in the green onions, add the thyme, basil and Creole seasoning to the vegetables. (The Creole seasoning is a mixture of salt and cayenne pepper. Use this seasoning sparingly until you have tasted the finished Jambalaya dish. Additional seasoning can be added later.)

Add the cooked sausage to the vegetables and sauté for 10 minutes. Remove the cooked chicken from the stock and pick the chicken meat.

In your stock pot combine 4 cups of chicken stock, uncooked rice, chicken meat, vegetables and sausage mixture. Cook until the rice is done. Stir often. The rice should absorb all of the chicken stock. If you need to add more water, do so sparingly so as not to make the rice mushy.

This dish is a good meal to freeze. It can be heated very easily in a microwave oven.

(Al and Clara May Haefner)

Vegetable

Grilled Asparagus

1 pound fresh asparagus
3 T. olive oil
¼ cup lemon juice
½ t. salt
¼ t. pepper

Snap off tough ends of asparagus. Drizzle asparagus with oil. Grill about 2 minutes on each side. Drizzle with lemon juice and sprinkle with salt and pepper. Cover and chill at least 2 hours.

Yields: 4 to 6 servings

(Greg Cannon)

Dessert

Strawberry Parfait

½ cup packed light brown sugar
3 T. raspberry or balsamic vinegar
2 cups sliced strawberries
strawberry sorbet
¼ cup crème fraiche
1½ t. sugar

To prepare strawberries: Combine brown sugar and vinegar in a medium bowl, stirring with a whisk. Add 2 cups strawberries, stirring gently to coat. Cover and chill 4 hours, stirring occasionally.

To prepare cream: Combine crème fraiche and 1½ t. sugar, stirring well until sugar dissolves. Cover and chill.

To assemble parfaits: Spoon 3 T. sorbet into each of 8 flutes; top with 3 T. strawberries. Spoon 1½ tablespoons cream over each serving. Drizzle remaining juices from the strawberries over each serving. Garnish with mint.

Yields 8

(Peter Thornton)

CONVERSATION

As they walked along, they were talking of Jesus' death, when suddenly Jesus joined them…and said, "you seem to be in deep conversation about something." (Luke 24:13-17)

Prayer: *I am giving Thee worship with my whole life, I am giving Thee assent with my whole power, I am giving Thee honor with my whole utterance, I am giving Thee reverence with my whole understanding, I am giving Thee offering with my whole thought, I am giving Thee praise with my whole fervor, I am giving Thee love with my whole devotion, I am giving Thee kneeling with my whole desire, I am giving Thee affection with my whole sense, I am giving Thee existence with my whole mind, I am giving Thee my soul, O God of all gods. (de Waal, THE CELTIC WAY OF PRAYER)*

- Cuisine Populaire: popular, economical meal of the day
- Cuisine Bourgeoise: elaborate and grand dining, celebrating luxury
- Cuisine du Terroir: the cuisine of the soil

Typical, fancy or basic…meat and potatoes, gourmet, or fresh garden food – it's the conversation that makes any meal special. Martin Luther labeled it table talk. What his wife, Katie, served didn't determine the quality of the theological discussion with family and guests.

It was cuisine populaire, broiled fish, served by Jesus to the remaining eleven original disciples the evening of His resurrection (Luke 24:42). Cuisine du terroir, the staple of wheat become bread, was part of the fare offered the Master to Cleopas and friend earlier the same day in the village of Emmaus (Luke 24:30). Levi, the just-retired tax collector, surely decided on cuisine bourgeoise for the reception honoring the Lord (Luke 5:29). Whether with two sad followers in Emmaus, eleven frightened men in a Jerusalem room, or a host of society's movers and shakers – many quite critical of Jesus – at Levi's upscale home…eating broiled fish, bread or catered hors d'oeuvers: Who would suggest the conversation with God's Son was better simply because of the place or menu? Small or large food budgets, china or paper plates, dining out or in, are irrelevant. Conversation about, and with, Jesus enlivens and blesses the table.

Or, as Craig A. Satterlee, Professor of Homiletics at the Lutheran School of Theology at Chicago, puts it:

> The risen Christ breaks bread in Emmaus and then eats fish in Jerusalem. Easter,
> or at least the first Easter as Luke describes it, is not as much about an empty tomb
> as about food. Jesus spends Easter day eating. His followers celebrate Easter not at
> an empty tomb, but around a table. So we might consider Easter as a multicourse meal
> rather than a trip to the empty tomb, and experience resurrection by eating.
> (CHRISTIAN CENTURY, April 18, 2006)

Ponderable

"Time is swift and glorious. Friendship is one of the few condiments that makes life both sweet and sour."
(Eugene Walter in the Pat Conroy Cookbook – Recipes Of My Life)

GRACE
Romans 4:20-26

Prayer: *What we ask of Thee wisely, O God, do Thou of Thy great bounty bestow; with all that we so deeply need and know not how to ask: that in the knowledge of Thy love we may have the peace that comes not of our striving but of Thy gift. Through Jesus Christ, our Lord. Amen. (Paul Scherer, LOVE IS A SPENDTHRIFT, 1961)*

I was not able to determine the scripture reference noted in her restaurant's name, grace / 1720, until I checked the website (www.grace1720.com):

> Jesus said to them, "Truly I say to you, if you have faith as a grain of mustard seed,
> you will say to this mountain, 'Move from here to there,' and it will move; and
> nothing will be impossible to you." (Matthew 17:20)

Chef and owner Barbara DiJames adds, "Opening our restaurant was quite a leap of faith!" Her advertisement includes,

> **"Grace (grāce) n.**
> seemingly effortless beauty or charm of movement, form or proportion;
> an excellence or power granted by God;
> a short prayer of blessing or thanksgiving said before or after a meal;
> a fine restaurant in Norcross, Georgia."

Nice touch, don't you think?

But how about this one reported by Rebecca Mead in THE NEW YORKER (March 21, 2005),

> Diners browsing their options on Macdougal Street in the Village might be surprised
> that Babu has a menu that comes without prices. Instead, guests are invited to eat,
> enjoy, and then, at the end of the meal, pay what they thought it was worth…The
> pay-what-you-like policy has caused a certain amount of anxiety among diners…
> The problem is a lack of an established code of behavior to follow.

Wow! That strikes at the heart of the struggle of many Christians I know who are caught up in the question of salvation by grace and faith in Jesus (Romans 4) or by good works (James 2:14-18) – a restored relationship with God through trusting in Jesus' promises, or by proving we are "saved" by the holiness of our lives?

The spiritual wrestling match for a host of my friends is between the lack of an established code of behavior to follow (rules and regulations and how many divine points do I get for this good work?), verses indicating that God's love in Jesus is on the house (a gift of a new quality of life that cannot be earned), unmerited, undeserved. Grace: the Lord's menu without prices…that "comes not of our striving but of Thy gift."

Blessed are we who realize that, Biblically speaking, salvation by grace (faith) goes hand-in-hand with good works (living the Christ-dictated life). What confuses some seems to be which precedes the other. Scripture is clear: accept the Gift, then respond with a life lived as our "thank you" that pleases the Master.

Ponderable

Love is a spendthrift, leaves its arithmetic at home, is always "in the red." And God is love.
(The late Paul Scherer, of Holy Trinity Lutheran Church, New York City, and beloved Professor of Homiletics when I was a student at Princeton Theological Seminary)

WINE
Romans 14

Prayer: *Grant, we pray, a Spirit in Your Church that allows hidden things to be revealed to us, and new ways found to touch the hearts of all. May we preserve with each other sincere charity and peace, and, if it be Your holy will, grant that this place of Your abiding be continued still to be a sanctuary and a light, through Jesus Christ. Amen. (IONA ABBEY WORSHIP BOOK, Scotland's Iona Community, 2001)*

Insights from the Scriptures can be paradoxical. Not contradictory. In a paradox one or both perspectives may be true or false at the same time. In a contradiction, one is true, the other false.

Consider some paradoxical verses about wine, and be reminded of the danger inherent in "proof texting," (lifting a verse, usually out of context, to prove one's prejudice).

- The Lord spoke to Aaron, 'Drink no wine nor strong drink, you nor your sons, when you go into the tent of meeting, lest you die....' (Leviticus 10:8-9)

- Thou, O God, dost cause grass to grow for the cattle, and plants for man to cultivate...and wine to gladden the heart of man....(Psalm 104:14-15)

- Wine is mocker, strong drink a brawler; and whoever is led astray by it is not wise. (Proverbs 20:1)

- Eat your bread with enjoyment, and drink your wine with a merry heart; for God has already approved what you do. (Ecclesiastes 9:7)

- There was a marriage at Cana in Galilee....Jesus was there....The wine failed.... Jesus transformed water into wine for the wedding reception guests. (John 2:1-11)

- Who has woe, sorrow, strife? Those who tarry long over wine....(Proverbs 23:29-30)

- St. Paul to Timothy: "No longer drink only water, but use a little wine for the sake of your stomach and your frequent ailments." (I Timothy 5:23)

Footnote: In Europe, St. Martin's Day marks the official first day of the wine season. Anointed as the patron saint of grape growers, St. Martin's Day is celebrated on his birthday – it's an anniversary for all to share their bounty, feast on autumn foods and drink the new red wines. St. Martin himself set the pattern for sharing when, as a dashing young soldier at the gates of Amiens, he divided his cloak with a beggar. (NAPA STYLE catalogue)

Once upon a time I was being considered as the new Minister for our Presbyterian Church in a smaller western Pennsylvania college town. It appeared the Pastor Nominating Committee was prepared to invite me, and I felt I would accept the position...until the final meeting. That's when the chairperson explained to me that the congregation's "beloved former pastor" of some thirty years preached, at least annually, that the Bible demanded abstinence...that scripture's references to wine really were to fruit of the vine, unfermented grape juice. I recall thinking, "That's a creative reading of the written Word!" She then asked, in light of Dr. So-and-So's teaching, a question that startled me: Would I sign a pledge, as their new Head of Staff, not to consume alcoholic beverages?

Perhaps I should have paused briefly, as a courtesy, before responding, "No...and I'd like to tell you why." Without the Committee's permission, I pressed on to acknowledge I knew full well all the dangers involved with alcohol's misuse...that fruit of the vine doesn't necessarily yield drunkenness (about which the Bible is unanimously opposed)...that our Lord apparently imbibed (why else would Jesus note, in Matthew 11:18-19, that some of His critics labeled Him a glutton and drunkard)...and that, for me, the crux of the matter is found in Romans 14.

Before I could be interrupted, I lectured on. I was, at that time, Dean of the Chapel and Associate Professor of Religion at a nearby Presbyterian college, used to delivering classroom lectures. To spare you a lecture, kind reader, I believe St. Paul's position in Romans 14 can be summarized like this: Christians have a responsibility to never do anything that may cause another believer to stumble.

A rich New Testament Greek word, "skandalon", can be translated, "stumbling-block, to provide an occasion to fall, trip someone up, lure one into sin." Much is allowed in the Christian walk, but not all things are helpful to the believer and to others.

Sip your wine if you will (and do heed the T-shirt's admonition, Life's Too Short To Drink Cheap Wine), but woe to the one whose drinking causes another to stumble.

Ponderable

Dennis Burke, writing in the April 7, 1995 issue of COMMONWEAL, tells of a homily delivered during Mass at San Francisco's Holy Redeemer Church.

This is the kernel of what the priest said: "A man had a vineyard in the Napa Valley that had just been attacked by fungus. So he went to his son and said: 'Chablis, will you help me in the vineyard?' Chablis answered: 'Yes, of course.' But Chablis, distracted by friends, got in his red sports car, drove down to San Francisco, and was never heard from again." [spontaneous laughter] "The man went to his other son. 'Zinfandel,' [more laughter] 'will you help me in the vineyard?' Zinfandel replied: 'No, I'm busy.' Zinfandel walked away, but had second thoughts. [long pause] He returned and worked the vineyard.'
"God is in our second thoughts," the frail priest explained. "Not in the temptations that draw us or the impulses that propel us to what is wrong. No, God is in those brief moments before we decide to act; those moments when we catch ourselves considering things; those moments we call…second thoughts. So, at the Safeway store as you look over the wine aisle this week, ask yourself: 'When the temptations swirl around me, will it be Chablis or…' [long pause] 'Zinfandel?' "

Soup

Black-Eyed Pea and Sausage Soup

1 pound smoked sausage, sliced
2 teaspoons vegetable oil
1 large onion, chopped
3 carrots, coarsely chopped
3 garlic cloves, minced
2 celery ribs, chopped
1 large green bell pepper, chopped
4 cups frozen black-eyed peas (about 1-1/2 16 oz. packages)
3 (14-1/2 oz.) cans beef broth
1 (14-1/2 oz.) can diced tomatoes with basil, garlic
and oregano, undrained
1 (16 oz.) jar chipotle-flavored salsa
1/2 teaspoon salt
1/4 teaspoon pepper

Cook sausage in oil in a large Dutch oven, stirring until it browns. Remove sausage, reserving drippings in pan. Add onion and next 4 ingredients; sauté over medium-high heat 8 minutes or until vegetables are tender. Stir in sausage, peas, broth and tomatoes; bring to a boil. Cover, reduce heat and simmer 35 minutes. Stir in salsa, salt and pepper; simmer 10 more minutes. Serves 12.

(Ed Albright)

Appetizer

Marinated Goat Cheese with Sundried Tomatoes

1-2 cups extra virgin olive oil
10 peppercorns
1 t. rosemary
1 t. sage
1 t. thyme
3-4 whole garlic cloves, peeled
½ cup sundried tomatoes
2 small goat cheese logs

Combine ½ cup oil, pepper, herbs and garlic in pan. Heat until warm. Cool. Put tomatoes on bottom of dish. Put goat cheese on tomatoes. Place rest of tomatoes around goat cheese. Pour olive oil, herbs and garlic over cheese, then more olive oil to cover. Marinate in cool place. Serve on crackers. Yield: 20
(Jane Robinson)

Sauce

Remoulade Sauce

2 cups Hellman's mayonnaise
1 cup catsup
1 cup thinly sliced green onions, tops and bottoms
1 cup chopped celery
1 medium green pepper, thinly sliced
1 medium onion, chopped
1 cup horseradish
3 tablespoons lemon juice
3 tablespoons Lea & Perrin Worcestershire sauce
1 tablespoon dried basil
2 bay leaves
1/2 cup white wine vinegar
2 large cloves of garlic, pressed
3 tablespoons Tabasco sauce
salt and pepper

Mix well and set in refrigerator; will keep for a week to ten days. Serve over boiled shrimp or lettuce as a dressing; makes 1/2 gallon.

(Mike and Karen Zobrist)

FUN
The Preacher (Ecclesiastes)

Prayer: *Lord, help me to do great things as though they were little, since I do them with Your power; and little things as though they were great, since I do them in Your name. Amen. (Blaise Pascal, French Mathematician, Physicist, and Christian, 1623-1662)*

Ann founded and maintains the Morningstar Organic Farmer's Market in the Highlands section of Atlanta. Saturday mornings, during the season, she persuades some of the area's most talented chefs to offer a 9:30 a.m. cooking demonstration using the Market's produce. Quite fun for us kitchen rookies.

Using a bowl and mortar to demonstrate how to make the basic French mayonnaise, aioli (slices of fresh garlic, kosher salt, egg, slowly drizzled extra virgin olive oil), the chef of the morning commented,

> Cooking for me is cathartic. The fun is in the blending, mixing,
> and preparing, more than it is in plating the food.

When I felt a need to analyze why cooking is a fun hobby for me, I reasoned that its primary appeal is a sense of immediate satisfaction. Much of what I do as a parish pastor does not produce quick results. I teach and preach, counsel and administrate, and wait…and wait for tangible, measurable results. But plan a menu; grocery shop; prepare; serve; hear "That was delicious;" clean up: completed; accomplished; right now. Fun!

Rich Steves, host on the Public Broadcast Travel Channel, observed from Burgundy,

> To the French, eating is sacred but fun.

Cannot our Christian walk be the same? A sacred journey, of course, but fun, too. Relaxed reverence is the term I use when asked to explain my understanding of corporate public worship. "Lighten up" a bit, child of God, I frequently want to counsel. Reverent and relaxed. Believers should, I suggest, be fun to be with.

My dad, also a Presbyterian minister, taught me to revise slightly the first question and answer of the Westminster Shorter Catechism:

> Q. What is man's chief end?
> A. Man's chief end is to glorify God and enjoy Him forever."
> (…and have a good time doing it.)

I think dad was right. If you'll come by my Pastor's Study, I'd like to show you my favorite artistic guess of Jesus' face. It is titled The Laughing Christ.

Fun…one mark of a Christian.

Ponderable

> Go, eat your bread with enjoyment, and drink your wine with a merry
> heart; for God has already approved what you do. (Ecclesiastes 9:7)
>
> I know that there is nothing better for them than to be happy and enjoy
> themselves as long as they live; also that it is God's gift to man that every one
> should eat and drink and take pleasure in all his toil. (Ecclesiastes 3:12-13)
>
> **Neatest Trick Of The Week**
>
> (From a BOSTON GLOBE obituary of the chef and author Edna Lewis,
> THE NEW YORKER, March 20, 2006)
> Ms. Lewis grew up in Virginia on her family's farm, and she described the dinners
> she made from things she harvested in the books she later wrote.

TRAINING
Exodus 12

Prayer: *Most powerful Holy Spirit, come down upon us and subdue us. From heaven, where the ordinary is made glorious, and glory seems but ordinary, bathe us with the brilliance of Your light like dew. ("Celtic Daily Prayer," PRAYERS AND READINGS FROM THE NORTHUMBRIA COMMUNITY)*

Walking the aisles of Whole Foods Market, tempted at nearly every step by the variety and quality of their products (though pricey), I noticed a dad with his shopping cart followed by his young daughter pushing her own miniature cart. Attached on a pole, resembling a flag, was the notice, "Customer In Training." Aren't we all.

Sally discovered the spot and made reservations for us (Dee and Heather, Greg and Peter, Dorothy and me) at Atlanta's Le Cordon Bleu College of Culinary Arts. It is a restaurant named Lumiere (to illuminate, shed light upon)…with an open kitchen where students prepare and serve meals under the guidance of talented instructors. Chefs in training.

Learning by doing almost always tops learning by hearing. Read the cookbooks and attend the culinary classes, but the best education comes by taking whisk in hand, heating the cast iron skillet and dicing Louisiana's "trinity" (green peppers, onions and celery). " Lumiere, illuminate, shed light upon," by chefs-in-training doing food preparation.

The Bible's most central meal, Passover, found Jesus teaching more by action than words (John 13). The way Mark (chapter 14) recalls the memorable meal, the table already had been set by two disciples for the Feast of Unleavened Bread, likely similar to the contemporary Seder ceremony that helps re-tell the story of Passover: roasted egg; horseradish or onion root; shank bone of a lamb; mixture of apples, cinnamon and nuts; greens dipped in salt water.

Jesus begins the liturgy by stripping and wrapping a bath towel around His waist. With a bowl of water, the Master astonishes His closest friends by getting on His knees to wash their dusty, smelly feet.

I tried it once. Only once. Ash Wednesday, 1976; North Sewickley Presbyterian Church, Ellwood City, Pennsylvania; six Elders in active service; on the chancel steps. I didn't strip, nor did I really wash, just poured water over their feet, then dried them. Still, it was embarrassing for all of us. We understood Peter's protest, "Lord, You shall never wash my feet!"

When the two women and four men returned to their pews, I preached my briefest ever sermon. Few words were required. The message was in the example.

> Jesus said, "I, your Lord and Teacher, have washed your feet. You also ought
> to wash another's feet. I have given you an example….A new commandment
> I give you: Love one another as I have loved you. Everyone will know you are
> My disciples if you have love for one another."

Biblically speaking, love is a verb (action), not an adjective (feeling). "I have given you an example." If you are in training, I hear Jesus saying,

> As My follower, remember that talk is cheap. They will know you are
> one of Mine by your example, action,…by your love for one another.

Ponderable

The name Le Cordon Bleu (meaning Blue Ribbon) is rich with history and heritage. It has been synonymous with excellence since 1578, when King Henry III created "L'Ordre des Chevaliers du Saint Espirit" (the Order of the Holy Spirit). It was an exclusive Order in France until 1789. The members, royalty included, were ordained with the Cross of the Holy Spirit, which hung from a blue ribbon; they were called "Cordon Bleus."   (From Lumiere's menu)

FASTING

Prayer: *God, be merciful to me, a sinner. Amen. (Luke 18:13b)*

- "David and his men tore their clothes in sorrow when they heard the news of the deaths of Saul and his son, Jonathan. They mourned and wept and fasted all day….David refused to eat anything the day of Abner's funeral….David begged the Lord to spare Bathsheba's baby, and went without food and lay all night before the Lord on the bare earth." (II Samuel 1:11-12; 3:35; 12:16)

- "When they were ill, I mourned before the Lord in sackcloth, asking Him to make them well; I refused to eat; I prayed for them with utmost earnestness, but God did not listen." (Psalm 35:13)

- "Paul and Barnabas also appointed elders in every church and prayed for them with fasting, turning them over to the care of the Lord in Whom they trusted." (Acts 14:23)

- "When you fast, decline your food for a spiritual purpose; don't do it publicly, as the hypocrites do, who try to look wan and disheveled so people will feel sorry for them….Instead, put on festive clothing so that no one will suspect you are hungry, except your Father who knows every secret. And He will reward you." (Matthew 6:16-17)

- "One day the disciples of John the Baptist came to Jesus and asked Him, 'Why don't Your disciples fast as we do, and as the Pharisees do?' Jesus asked, 'Should the bridegroom's friends mourn and go without food while he is with them? But the time is coming when I will be taken from them. Time enough for them to refuse to eat.'" (Matthew 9:14-15) "Besides, going without food is part of the old way of doing things." (Mark 2:21)

- "Anna, a prophetess, was also there in the Temple that day….She was very old….She never left the Temple…worshiping God day and night by praying and often fasting." (Luke 2:36-37)

- "Two men went to the Temple to pray. One was a proud, self-righteous Pharisee; the other, a cheating tax collector. The Pharisee offered this prayer: 'Thank God, I'm not a sinner like everyone else, especially like that tax collector over there! I never cheat. I don't commit adultery. I go without food twice a week, and I give to God a tenth of everything I earn'…." Jesus said, "The tax-collecting sinner returns home forgiven; not the Pharisee." (Luke 18:10-14)

"Going without food is part of the old way of doing things," said God's Savior (Mark 2:21). The Law of Moses required fasting once annually in connection with the Day of Atonement, the twenty-fifth day of September,
This is a permanent law:

" on that day you must do no work, but must spend the day in self-examination and fasting." (Leviticus 16:29)

Biblical fasting was used in times of danger, sadness and calamities. At its best, the spiritual discipline of fasting is, scripturally, intended to demonstrate a change of heart in regard to God, self, and/or others.

In the introduction of his book of powerful meditations titled GETHSEMANI HOMILIES, Matthew Kelty, O.C.S.O., a Roman Catholic monk at the Abbey of Gethsemani, Kentucky, is interviewd by his editor, William O. Paulsell. (Stephen, one of my gifted colleagues in ministry at McDonough Presbyterian, made me the present of this book upon his return from a retreat at the Abbey.)

(Mr. Paulsell): "Was fasting more rigorous in your younger days as a monk?"

(Father Kelty): "Yes, less to eat. Fasting in my book is a disaster, it just doesn't work for me.
You just had coffee and bread in the morning and you dipped the coffee out of a big cauldron.
It would be steaming because the refectory had no heat. I was hungry all day. A huge meal at
noon of soup and vegetables, but 2:00 I would be famished. Supper would be a piece of
cheese and another piece of bread and some fruit. It was all right; you got enough to eat. One
main meal a day was the idea. Only the softies took anything in the morning. That was for the
chicken-hearted, those that had no guts. It is the same, only now you can get more in the morning and more
in the evening. It's not as grim as it was."

That's my kind of clergy: tell the truth straight-out, no sugar-coating it! "Disastrous" as fasting is and though it "just doesn't work" for him, it appears the devoted monk does so anyway! Why?

I'm guessing, naturally, since Father Kelty doesn't tell us. I suspect it has a great deal to do with discipline. Certainly there are dimensions of our Christian walk to which we adhere even if we don't much care for them, whether they work for us or not. We might call it duty.

Never tried fasting myself. It's very low on my "to do" list at the moment. But if it gets moved higher, I'll be sure the motivation is not to lose weight…not done publicly (Matthew 6)…and not as a play to earn God's favor "the old way" (Mark 2:21).

Ponderable

"Jesus loved to compare the Kingdom of God to a party. He would demonstrate the open border of the Kingdom of God by hosting or participating in parties where even the most notorious outcasts and sinners were welcome. Jesus was often criticized for this 'table fellowship' with notorious sinners; His critics assumed that Jesus' acceptance of these people implied an approval and endorsement of their shabby behavior. But they misunderstood: Jesus wanted to help them experience transformation. Rejection hardens people, but acceptance makes transformation possible. By accepting and welcoming people into His presence just as they were, with all their problems and imperfections, Jesus was exposing them…to the fact that transformation comes from being in interactive relationships with God and others."

(Brian D. McLaren, The Secret Message Of Jesus, 2006

Entrée

Chicken Mediterranean

1/2 pound skinned and boned chicken breast halves, cut into cubes
4 garlic cloves, minced
2 Tbsp. olive oil
1 (14-1/2 oz.) can diced tomatoes, undrained
1/4 cup kalamata olives, pitted and chopped
1/2 tsp. dried parsley
1/2 tsp. dried basil
1/2 tsp. dried oregano
1/3 cup feta
4 oz. penne pasta, cooked

Combine first 3 ingredients in a heavy-duty Ziploc plastic bag. Seal and chill 2 hours.

Cook chicken mixture in a skillet over medium-high heat 8 minutes, or until chicken is done; remove from skillet. Add tomatoes and next 4 ingredients to skillet. Reduce heat and simmer, stirring often, 7 minutes. Return chicken to skillet. Sprinkle with feta cheese and remove from heat. Cover and let stand 5 minutes. Serve over hot pasta.

Yield: 2 servings

To serve 4, double all ingredients except diced tomatoes.

(Bobby and Jean Foster)

Dessert

Shortbread

1½ cups sifted flour
2 sticks butter, softened
¾ cup confectioner's sugar
¼ tsp. salt

Mix all ingredients together. Knead until well mixed and smooth. Press into lightly greased pan or shortbread mold. Bake at 325°F approximately 45 minutes. Shortbread should be pale brown in color. If it gets too brown, it's bitter.

(Sherry Galloway)

Salad

Sensation Dressing

1/2 cup vegetable oil
1/2 cup olive oil
2-1/2 tablespoons lemon juice
1-1/2 tablespoons vinegar
3/4 teaspoon salt
1 cup Romano cheese, grated
1/4 cup bleu cheese, crumbled
lettuce
parsley (chopped)
grated black pepper to taste

Mix first six ingredients for dressing. Tear lettuce and lots of parsley. Toss greens until well coated. Sprinkle bleu cheese and Romano cheese over greens and toss again. Add grated black pepper over salad.

Yield: 1-1/4 cups: enough for 2 large heads of lettuce

(Peggy Hammond)

TAKE AWAY
Luke 2:1-19

Prayer: *Lord, I know not what I ought to ask of Thee; Thou only knowest what I need; Thou lovest me better than I know how to love myself. O Father! Give to Thy child that which he himself knows not how to ask. I dare not ask either for crosses or consolations: I simply present myself before Thee; I open my heart to Thee. Behold my needs which I know not myself; see and do according to Thy tender mercy. Smite, or heal; depress me, or raise me up: I adore all Thy purposes without knowing them; I am silent; I offer myself in sacrifice: I yield myself to Thee; I would have no other desire than to accomplish Thy will. Teach me to pray. Pray Thyself in me. Amen. (Francois Fenelon, 18th century spiritual giant)*

There I was very early Christmas morning, trying to figure out which one of the three lines leading to a seat on Southwest Airline's flight from Ft. Lauderdale to Jacksonville, Florida, was the shortest. I could barely wait to get home to Mrs. Rose. In anticipation, I slept little after the midnight Christmas Eve Service I conducted as their Interim Head of Staff at West Kendall's Central Presbyterian Church.

Dorothy and I had agreed that we would experiment with her staying in Jacksonville to work in a middle school media center while I took up residence in a Miami-area apartment for a year or so. Only a strong, satisfying, happy marriage allows such an arrangement. The contract I negotiated with the gracious leaders of the Church had me work fourteen days followed by four days off, with the congregation generously paying to either fly Dorothy to Miami or me home. As rough as it was to be separated that much (our phone bill was astronomical), the reward was a wonderful "honeymoon" about twice a month.

Between the early Christmas Eve Service and the later one, Jay stopped by my Pastor's Study with a Christmas gift: a cookbook, autographed by Jo Ann Bass, from Joe's Stone Crab Restaurant (where Jay once worked) and two dozen very expensive stone crabs packed in dry ice in the restaurant's famous Take Away container. Immediately I phoned Dorothy: There's a change of plans for our Christmas lunch!

For the uneducated: No one knew, until the 1920's, that the delicacy called stone crab claws was even edible. The crustacean is found along the coast from North Carolina to Mexico, but is commercially harvested (October 16-May 14), mostly in Florida, and consumer demand usually exceeds the supply. Captured in baited trays, only one claw can be removed (at one of the joints, to prevent bleeding) so the crab can defend itself. Four inches from the first joint to the tip is the minimum size (about two ounces). During the life of the crab, the same appendage may be generated three or four times, taking a year or so to again reach legal size. The claw is cooked (7-8 minutes) in boiling water, cracked with a wooden mallet and served with clarified lemon butter or, my favorite, Joe's famous mustard sauce.

My container caused quite a stir in the terminal: Are those really stone crabs?....from Joe's?....What a treat!....Would you consider selling some to me?....Guard them with your life! I made more "friends" in a half-hour or so that early Christmas morning than ever before! It was announced over the plane's PA system, by a flight attendant, with the lightheartedness typical of Southwest, that a passenger might be willing to auction off some Joe's Stone Crabs if the price was right.

During what felt like an unbearably long flight, anticipating Dorothy and the stone crabs, the preacher in me fell to thinking about this unusual experience as it might relate to the sermon I delivered a few hours earlier. The thrust of the Christmas Eve late service's message was that God regularly uses some unexpected (startling, really) means to reveal Herself. After all, who could imagine the promised Messiah showing up in a barn rather than the Bethlehem Hilton; parented by a strangely matched couple but sired by God; birth announced primarily to religious outcasts of the day as they tried to stay awake to protect their sheep; a journey guided by the strangest of stars; et. al. But, of course, the account has held the world's attention for centuries.

I had the attention of a bunch of folks in the terminal and airplane because of a strange Christmas gift I carried, and never used the Take Away container to reveal a glimpse of our Gift-Giving God. It would have been so easy, so natural, so non-threatening to say: Yeah, a fellow at Church gave them to me....Jay said it was a reminder of how generous God's giving is, giving us the Gift of Jesus.... Who knows – to Christ's glory – where the conversations might have gone?

Ponderable

A Celtic prayer as we meet others:
The joy of God be in thy face,
Joy to all who see thee,
The circling of God be keeping thee,
Angels of God be shielding thee.
(Carmina Gadelica)

HELPERS
I Corinthians 12:27-13:8

Prayer: *As Brigid, with a cross of rushes, comforted a stranger; empower us to take into daily life signs of Your divine healing and hope. As Patrick traveled ever on; as Margaret built community; so may we reach beyond ourselves to share the lives of others, and touch a wider world. Amen (Iona Abbey Worship Book, Scotland's Iona Community, 2001)*

My fledgling comprehension of New Testament Greek prevents me from knowing exactly what "helpers" means as St. Paul lists them in I Corinthians 12. Guesses about the role of apostles, prophets, teachers, miracle workers, et. al., in the Church are easier. Seldom are helpers lifted up as significant players in Christ's ministry. Typically it's the other spiritual leaders who get the headlines.

I wonder if the Greek word "splagchnizesthai" may apply, at least in part, to helpers. It means "to be moved with compassion." I'm thinking of the host of helpers – at least seventy-five daily for eight days – who were "moved by compassion" to assist survivors of Hurricane Katrina whose temporary escape was to Henry County, Georgia, where the congregation I serve as Minister is about the Lord's work.

Early in September of 2005, our church facilities became the major distribution center for goods and services to refugees in our community from the Gulf Coast. Originally the Red Cross was to staff it. For reasons that never have been explained to me, they didn't kept their word. An estimated 16,000 people received two complete hot meals daily prepared on site in our commercial kitchen…tons of basic food items…medical attention, including more than $40,000 in prescriptions and $8,000 for eye care…counseling…temporary housing…gasoline vouchers…financial assistance (it was quite a sight when a helicopter, carrying two million dollars to distribute, landed on one of our ballfields…security for our President couldn't have been more thorough)…and perhaps most significantly, a caring, Christian welcome as our guests.

I later received a clipping from the Gainesville Sun that quoted Audrey, vice-president of a homeowner's association in Ocala, Florida, reminding residents that they were prohibited from taking hurricane refugees into their homes, writing...

"These are single-family residences, and that's what they are intended for."

To the group's credit, the residents were encouraged to donate to charity instead.

We felt differently at McDonough Presbyterian. A major justification for spending $3.5 million renovating and expanding our church plant a couple of years earlier was to equip us to better serve the needs of our community. Few, if any, imagined that our new gym and Sunday School rooms, hallways, ballfields, and bathrooms would ever try to accommodate such a throng.

We did (though it was controlled chaos), and about $10,000 worth of damage to the facilities resulted. I never heard a word of complaint from our membership.

I mentioned how a host of faith-based and community organizations extended a "caring, Christian welcome" to the 16,000 evacuees. That was Mike Turner's doing. Director of Public Safety for Henry County, he took control of operations when it became apparent the Red Cross was not going to. With "grace under pressure" and gentle humor, Mike reminded us constantly,

> These people have been through a lot. They deserve the best care we can provide.
> Think of yourself as a concierge in a fancy hotel whose responsibility it is to
> assist guests in any way possible. And these folks are our special guests.

Helpers…moved with compassion.

When Georgia's Governor and First Lady, Mary, arrived by helicopter to see our ministry first-hand, Sonny Perdue told me, "I can't imagine how what you are doing could be done any better."

Recognition, awards, and plaques from the Henry County Chamber of Commerce, Henry County Board of Commissioners, National Association for the Advancement of Colored People, Georgia Department of Human Resources, as well as newspaper features followed. But the kudos that matter most come from God's Son to all helpers,

> Then those goats are going to say, "Master, what are You talking about? When did
> we ever see you hungry or thirsty or homeless or shivering or sick or in prison and
> didn't help?" He will answer them, "I'm telling the solemn truth: Whenever you
> failed to do one of these things to someone who was being overlooked or ignored,
> that was Me – you failed to do it to Me." (Matthew 25:37-40, Peterson)

Ponderable

> It's not the critic who counts; not the man who points out how the strong man stumbles,
> or where the doer of deeds could have done better. The credit belongs to the man who
> is actually in the arena…who, at best, knows in the end the triumph of great achievement,
> and who, at the worst, if he fails, at least fails while daring greatly. So that his place will
> never be with those cold, timid souls who know neither victory or defeat.
> (Theodore Roosevelt)

UNANSWERED
Psalm 22:1-2

**Table
Grace:**

Thank Thee, Our Father, for our food, and all Thy gifts, for they are good. Amen.
(Stuart R. Oglesby, Prayers For All Occasions, 1940)

For a local lunch, I don't think you can top the food, service and price at Truman's, just off McDonough's square. Chef David, the owner and one of my cooking mentors, along with his staff, do it right. There's a downside to dining at Truman's, however: You're bound to see neighbor, friends, acquaintances. That's nice, of course, unless you are in the mood to dine alone. Garrison Keillor explains, (Lake Wobegon Days, 1985)

Father Emil comes in for lunch. Harold: "Shhhh. If Father hears us talk, we'll be here till Tuesday." With Father is Father Willetz, visiting from St. Cloud, a priest who wears a turtleneck. Father stands by the coat rack, pretending to read the auction notices and ballroom posters. Actually he is scouting the room for the right place to sit, a strategic problem for a priest who simply wants to eat lunch and not necessarily be asked what he thinks about those Benedictines who got hold of St. Mary's in Finseth. St. Mary's was a gorgeous Church until the Benedictines came through and told people they ought to clean out the statuary and the high altar, which the people did, and do you know what they used for an altar? A lunch table! From the cafeteria! Set right out on the floor where everybody could see it – why? Why tear the Church apart so you can see the priest say Mass? Father Emil has been asked about St. Mary's often enough, by sitting near the wrong people at lunch who feel obliged to make conversation on holy things. He says a prayer, asking God to grant him a secular lunch.

Typical Garrison humor and insight. If you have qualms about praying for such a mundane matter as a secular lunch, consider rethinking the significance of Christ teaching disciples of all generations to include in His brief model prayer a petition for basic, ordinary, "daily bread." A "secular lunch" plea may, at least occasionally, be o.k.

I mentioned that David is one of my favorite food preparation mentors. I spent three hours once in his kitchen, chopping onions, squash, and cucumbers; making meatloaf, grilling bread, trimming asparagus. I also messed up one of Truman's basic spices (equal parts black pepper, kosher salt and garlic salt – I used garlic powder instead; David was gracious as he dumped it out and re-did it correctly). It is hectic, demanding work in a restaurant's kitchen.

The next time your meal out is so exceptional that you ask to speak to the chef so you can give her/him your compliments, I propose beginning with, "Please thank your dish/pot washer – I know they are the hardest workers in your kitchen."

The old country music song has a line, "Thank God for unanswered prayers." It's a story about a fellow at a high school football game with his wife. Running into an old flame he realizes his prayer that one day he and his senior high girlfriend would marry was best left unanswered. He is thankful to be the husband of his bride.

33

I once dreamed – nearly prayed about – owning a restaurant with my friend Bob, who schooled me in the art of selling the James Austin Company's household cleaning products to grocery store chains (at a time in my life when I had left the ministry). We fantasized about buying the railroad terminal in Columbus, Ohio, and turning it into a restaurant called Dudley's Depot (The menu would be "punched" by a "conductor"; food would be served on luggage carts, etc.). I thank God the dream was unanswered. I do so because my return to parish ministry is what I know God wanted and still wants me to do – and now I know how rough the food industry business is.

Do you dream that the grass is greener on the other side? Are you open to unanswered prayer, to the possibility that God intends, rather, for you to bloom where you are planted? It's not so much where we are…what we do…but who we are as Jesus' followers that is a key to fulfilled life as a Christian. I wonder if the Apostle Paul didn't have that in mind when he wrote,

> "I have learned by now to be quite content whatever my circumstances.
> Whatever I have, wherever I am, I can make it through anything in the
> One who makes me who I am."
> (Philippians 4:11-13, The Message, Eugene Peterson)

Ponderable

"My grace is enough for you." I suppose there are people who read those words and are far more sure than they ought to be that Paul really heard them! We could manage too, on such terms. He prayed once, and what he wanted didn't happen; so he prayed again, and it didn't happen then, either. We'll go along with that. That's exactly how it is. But the third time he got an answer, and we haven't had any. I can't help wondering about that. It's the silence, the terrible silence, that says "No" to us. I wonder if it wasn't the silence, the terrible silence, that said "No" to him – "No, but…?" He carried that burden all his life, you know. Some blemish, was it, that would make a Jew ashamed? The pride and the passion maybe that kept nagging at him all his days. Perhaps the secret of it lies hidden away somewhere in the agony of that seventh chapter of Romans: "The good that I would I do not: but the evil which I would not, that I do….O wretched man that I am! Who shall deliver me from the body of this death?" Then the doxology for a victory that hadn't been won yet: "I thank God through Jesus Christ our Lord." When you don't hear anything, isn't there something you ought to hear? "My grace is enough for you." (Paul Scherer, Love Is a Spendthrift, Meditations for the Christian Year, 1961)

ONE LINERS

"Write the vision; make it plain upon tablets, so he may run who reads it."
(Habakkuk 2:2)

Prayer: *May love with all things good be found, and grateful thanks to Thee abound. Amen. (Stuart R. Oglesby, Prayers for All Occasions, 1940)*

- l'art de vivre (the art of living).

- Before we can call Jesus Friend, we must call Him Lord.

- A tavola nun s'invecchia mai (At the table, no one gets old).

- Taste and see that the Lord is good. (Psalm 34:8)

- l'art de la table (the art of dining).

- The Gospel is often simple, but it is rarely obvious.

- La vivanda vera e l'animo e la sera (Authentic food is the spirit of the evening).

- Let the Jesus in me serve the Jesus in you. (Mother Teresa)

- Like meat, the world needs some fat to give it flavor.

- All scripture is a commentary on God in the Garden asking, "Where are you?" (William Willimon)

- The pleasures of eating and drinking operate on so many levels that hard and fast rules about pairing wine and food make no sense. (Oz Clarke)

- When God created man, God gave him a secret: not how to begin but how to begin again. (Elie Weisel)

- What grows well together cooks well together.

- Gnocchi, Italian for "dumpling," is a two, not three, syllable word: "Nok"" ("Hallowed" also is two syllables).

- When the truth becomes a casualty, God's prophet must speak.

- You grow up the day you have your first real laugh…at yourself. (Ethel Barrymore)

- The eye tastes the food before the palate does; presentation is important.

- There are two ways of spreading light: be the candle or the mirror that reflects it. (Ethel Wharton)

- I have never heard a sermon from which I have not derived some good, but there have been many near misses. (Mark Twain)

Ponderable

There may be no better service a preacher can render on Easter morning than to resist hyperbole and fly close to the ground, saying the bare minimum about what we can know and what we cannot, about where knowing runs out and faith begins, about what is our business and what belongs to God alone.

I recently read a book review in which the author was praised for "leaving all the right things unsaid so that the silence resounds," and it occurred to me that we could use more silence in our sermons these days. By silence I do not mean the literal absence of speech, although that might not be a bad idea. I mean fewer, more carefully chosen words, with less presumption in them. I mean greater respect for the mystery of God which passes all understanding, and deeper humility about our own relative size in the universe.

(Barbara Brown Taylor, Episcopal priest, professor and preacher extraordinaire)

OIL
Exodus 30

Table Grace: *Give us grateful hearts, O God, for all Your mercies, and make us mindful of the needs of others, through Jesus Christ our Lord. Amen. (Daily Prayer – Supplemental Liturgical Resource 5, Presbyterian Church, USA)*

Olive oil, historically, has had more uses than one might imagine: as perfume, for embalming, as medicine, in cleansing, for massaging, as a cosmetic, and of course, in cooking. There are numerous renaissance paintings of Christ on the "Mount of Olives." Van Gogh's 1889 "Olive Trees" masterpiece, done at Saint-Remy, east of Paris, is one of these.

The ancient Maundy Thursday Mass included the consecration of oils,
We pray Thee, Lord, to bless this oil that Thou hast caused to be made by the
olive tree, that immortal tree, so that it may serve to heal the body and the soul.

Garden of Gethsemane, in Hebrew (Gat Shemen) translates as olive press. In the Greek Orthodox ritual, consecrated oil is used to anoint during Baptism and to illuminate altars and household icons. Also, it is burned during funeral services. (All the above from The Little Book of Olive Oil, Nicolas de Barry, translated by Louise Guiney.)

When we at McDonough Presbyterian offered a Service for Wholeness and Health, olive oil was available for anointing by Elders and Ministers. Exodus 30 gives a detailed recipe for making a holy anointing oil. Noah's dove returned to the Ark bearing an olive branch. Some Christians carry not only palms but branches of olives in the Palm Sunday procession. There are Biblical scholars who think Jesus' cross, the Roman death chamber, was made of cedar and olive woods.

Dorothy and I keep an inexpensive and a costly olive oil in our kitchen. Both are always "extra virgin" and "cold pressed." Some of the best comes from Spain, the world's leading producer, and we use it for salad dressing (combined with a top-notch balsamic vinegar; three parts oil to one part vinegar), to make pesto, and as a "topping" drizzled, just before presentation, over dishes such as fish. The cheaper oil we use for sautéing and other cooking. Olive oil (never to be refrigerated) stays freshest in a metal or dark container (light can damage its quality). Unlike wine, olive oil does not improve with age, so hasten to enjoy it.

I learned from the above mentioned book that like all fruit trees, olive trees require pruning – annually if possible – in order to obtain a maximum yield. (They produce fruit only once every two years.) Three types of pruning are used. The first two methods have as their goal to allow light to penetrate, and to assure the fruits will be as near as possible to the trunk.   The third method is called "revival pruning," using a saw to cut off parts of an unproductive tree.

Jesus said, "By this my Father is glorified; that you bear much fruit, and so prove to be my disciples." (John 15:8)

Ponderable

I am the true vine, and My Father is the vinedresser. Every branch of Mine that bears not fruit, He takes away, and every branch that does bear fruit He prunes, that it may bear more fruit. (John 15:1-2)
In the beginning was the Word, and the Word was with God, and the Word was God. He was in the beginning with God; all things were made through Him, and without Him was not anything made that was made. In Him was life, and the life was the light of men. The light shines in the darkness, and the darkness has not overcome it. (John 1:1-5)
Abide in Me, and I in you. As the branch cannot bear fruit by itself, unless it abides in the vine, neither can you, unless you abide in Me. I am the vine, you are the branches. He who abides in Me, and I in him, he it is that bears much fruit, for apart from Me you can do nothing. (John 15:4-5)

If a man does not abide in Me, he is cast forth as a branch and withers; and the branches are gathered, thrown into the fire and burned. (John 15:6)

RIVALRY

His brothers took Joseph and cast him into a pit. Then they sat down to eat. (Genesis 37:24-25)

Prayer: *O Christ, the arms of Your cross stretch out across the broken world in reconciliation. You have made peace with us. Help us to make peace with You by sharing in Your reconciling work. Amen. (Iona Abbey Worship Book, Scotland's Iona Community, 2001)*

Sounds like something one expects from the old-time Sicilian mafia: "Welcome Alfonso! Sit. We'll pour the vino, roll the spaghetti. How are the children…the wife?….Alfonso, you have betrayed 'the family.' Bang! Bang!" (inspired by "The Sopranos")

Gratefully, the Genesis account of the sadistic event in the life of the 17-year-old dreamer, Joseph, is a little less graphic, though as chilling. (You may want to refresh your memory of all that precedes and follows verses 24 and 25 in Genesis chapter 37.) What has my attention at this moment is, "Then Joseph's brothers sat down to eat…" with the frightened voice of their youngest sibling, I imagine, pleading for help from the pit! Enjoy your picnic, boys! Pour the wine, munch on figs, share the cheese, pass the bread.

"Now Israel (Dad) loved Joseph more than any other of his children…
so his brothers hated Joseph…were jealous of him." (Genesis 37:3-4,11)

Three New Testament Greek words (with appreciation to William Barclay, New Testament Words, 1964), when strung together, suggest to me how one allows such a dastardly deed like the "pit" to happen.

eritheia: squabbles, jockeying for positions of power, selfish ambition.

 hubris: acting with wanton insolence, unbridled self-assertion, allowing the passions to rule, arrogant contempt which makes one trample on others.

porosis: hardening of the heart, loss of all feeling, blind insensitivities, one whose conscience has petrified.

All three, with hatred and jealousy added, result in rivalry that destroys families, damages relationships and devastates Jesus' Church.

Christ's challenge to rivalry is outlined in the multiple definitions of a fourth Greek New Testament term, *agape*. Dr. Barclay was a magnificent Scottish scholar and Biblical commentator. One of my most enduring meal memories is of sitting at a banquet in Scotland's St. Andrew's University while there for a brief period of study, as the haggis – minced heart and liver of a sheep with oatmeal, etc., boiled in the animal's stomach – was piped in and Barclay officiated at the series of straight Scotch toasts using the traditional "liturgy" of Bobby Burns. Barclay on *agape*,

What then is the meaning of this agape? The supreme passage for the interpretation
of the meaning of agape is Matthew 5:43-48. We are bidden to love our enemies. Why?
In order that we should be like God. And what is the typical action of God that is cited?
God sends His rain on the just and the unjust and on the evil and the good. That is to
say – no matter what a man is like, God seeks nothing but his highest good. Let a man
be a saint or let a man be a sinner, God's only desire is for that man's highest good. Now,
that is what agape is. Agape is the spirit which says: "No matter what any man does to
me, I will never seek to do harm to him; I will never set out for revenge; I will always seek
nothing but his highest good." That is to say, Christian love, agape, is unconquerable
benevolence, invincible good will. It is not simply a wave of emotion; it is a deliberate
conviction of the mind issuing in a deliberate policy of the life; it is a deliberate
achievement and conquest and victory of the will. It takes all of a man to achieve
Christian love; it takes not only his heart; it takes his mind and his will as well.

Ponderable

"Though we speak with the tongues of orators and of angels, but have no love, we are hollow-sounding foghorns or nerve-wracking rattles. And though we have the ability to preach, and know all the secrets and all the slogans, and though we have sufficient faith to move a mountain, but have no love, we are nothing. Even though we renounce all our possessions, and give our bodies as flaming sacrifices, but have no love, we accomplish exactly nothing.

Love is long-suffering and kind. Love is not envious, nor does it strut and brag. It does not act up, nor try to get things for itself. It pitches no tantrums, keeps no books on insults or injuries, sees no fun in wickedness, but rejoices when truth prevails. Love is all-embracing, all-trusting, all-hoping, all-enduring. Love never quits.

As for sermons, they shall be silenced; as for oratory, it shall cease; as for knowledge, it will vanish. For our knowledge is immature, and our preaching is immature; but when that which is mature arrives, it supercedes the immature.

For example, when I was a child, I was talking like a child, thinking like a child, acting like a child; but when I became an adult, I outgrew my childish ways. So, on the childish level – that is, without love – we look at one another in a trick mirror. But on the adult level – that is, with love – we see face to face. As children – that is, without love – we understand immaturely; but as adults – that is, with love – we'll understand just as we've been understood.

Now these three things endure: faith, hope and love; but the greatest of all is love. Amen."

(Clarence Jordan, The Cotton Patch Version; revised to eliminate sexist language)

Soup

Chicken and Andouille Sausage Gumbo

1 pound Andouille sausage, cut into 1/4 inch slices
3 boneless, skinless chicken breasts
3 boneless, skinless chicken thighs
1/4 cup olive oil
3/4 cup flour
1 medium onion, chopped
1/2 medium green pepper, chopped
2 celery ribs, sliced
3 garlic cloves, minced
4 cups water
4 cups chicken broth
1 tablespoon Creole seasoning
1/2 teaspoon dried thyme
1 teaspoon hot sauce
2 bay leaves
1/2 cup sliced green onions

Brown sausage in Dutch oven over medium heat, stirring until it is no longer pink. Reserve drippings in pan. Set sausage aside. Cut chicken breasts and thighs into 1-inch pieces and brown in hot drippings. Remove chicken, reserving drippings. Measure drippings, adding enough olive oil to measure 1/2 cup. Heat mixture in Dutch oven over medium-high heat until hot. Whisk in flour and cook, whisking constantly, 10-12 minutes or until roux is caramel colored. Add chopped onion and next 3 ingredients; cook until vegetables are tender. Gradually stir in 4 cups water and broth; bring to a boil. Add chicken, Creole seasoning and next 3 ingredients; reduce heat and simmer 30 minutes. Add sausage and green onions and cook 30 minutes. Remove and discard bay leaves; serve over rice.

Yield: 3 quarts

(Ruth Rucker)

Appetizer

Olive Crostini Baguette

1 can (4-1/2 oz.) black olives – chopped
1/2 cup pimiento stuffed olives – chopped
1/2 cup (2oz.) shredded parmesan cheese
4 T. butter – softened
2 garlic cloves – minced
3/4 cup (3 oz.) Monterey jack cheese – shredded
1/4 cup fresh parsley – chopped
French baguette – 1/4-inch slices

Mix all ingredients together; spread on baguette and broil.

Makes 25

(Lewis Robinson)

Slaw

Asian Slaw

2 (3 oz.) packages beef flavored ramen noodles
2 (8.5 oz.) packages slaw mix
1 cup sliced almonds, toasted
1 cup sunflower kernels
1 bunch green onions, chopped

1/2 cup sugar
3/4 vegetable oil
1/3 cup white vinegar

Remove flavor packets from noodles and put aside. Crush noodles and place in bottom of large bowl. Top with slaw. Sprinkle almonds, sunflower kernels and onions on top of slaw. Whisk the flavor packets with sugar, oil, and vinegar. Pour over slaw; cover and chill 2 hours (minimum). Toss before serving.

Yield: 10-12 servings

(Willene Stewart)

ROLES
I Corinthians 12

And they came to Capernaum; and when Jesus was in the house He asked them, "What were you discussing on the way?" But they were silent; for on the way they had discussed with one another who was the greatest. And He sat down and called the twelve; and Jesus said to them, "If any one would be first, he must be last of all and servant of all."

(Mark 9:33-35)

Prayer: *Dear God, may we know You more clearly, follow You more nearly, love You more dearly. Amen. ("Day by Day" – Godspell)*

During the writing of these chapters the death of 82-year-old William Sloan Coffin, due to congenital heart failure, was reported. The roles the exemplary modern Christian prophet carried out were astonishing in their variety. Bill Coffin (I recall little of what he said, but everything of his "presence," the evening I sat with twenty or so other believers at a "coffee and cookie time" in a Jacksonville, Florida, United Methodist Church parlor, following a presentation he made to a larger group earlier in the Sanctuary) served the God he loved as a CIA agent and as a leader in the 1960s' anti-Vietnam War protests. A Chaplain at Yale, he became active as a promoter of a White alliance with the Black movement for full equality. Though a child of the establishment, he became a spokesman for America's outcast. While Senior Minister of New York City's prestigious Riverside Church, he organized SANE-FREEZE in opposition to the ongoing development of nuclear weapons. He was a Presbyterian by training, but ecumenical by desire. Although he buried a son who was killed in his early twenties in a one-car accident, Coffin refused to give up on a God of love and compassion. A civil rights activist (Freedom Rider) made famous as Rev. Sloan in the Doonesbury comic strip, he remained gracious, approachable, gentle, and humble. (Some of the above phrases are from Roman Catholic priest James Carrol in his introduction to Credo.)

In light of the above, I reviewed my forty some years of ordained ministry, thinking specifically of my various roles; none as prominent or powerful as Dr. Coffin's list…but used by God nevertheless. It's something of what St. Paul meant when he wrote,

> There are varieties of gifts (from God), but the same Spirit (of God)….to each is given the
> manifestation of Jesus' Spirit for the common good….all are inspired by the same
> Divine Spirit who apportions to each one individually as He will….(1 Corinthians 12)

God has used me, to greater or lesser degrees of effectiveness for Kingdom causes, in roles as Pastor of rural, city, and suburban congregations, larger or smaller in membership…college Chaplain and Professor of Religion…football coach…certified Interim Minister…salesman…organizer of a new church development…speaker to gatherings hosted by the National Funeral Director's Association…pastoral counselor…Alban Institute-trained consultant in church conflict management… husband, father, and grandfather…author…son and brother.

There is no bragging intended in such a listing. Rather, the observation, and reminder, that whatever our roles as the Lord's followers, He creates abundant opportunities to "speak a good word for Jesus" in all of them. Even in my role these last six years as a bartender!

It's Kim and Jack's annual first-Saturday-of-December State Farm Christmas Open House, a perfect party: lavish without being ostentatious. Dorothy and I are thrilled to be on the guest list that now numbers more than two hundred. Not only invited, but given airline tickets to Bloomington, Illinois by our generous hosts. The "spread" is a gastronomical delight, some prepared by Kim (with Dorothy's late-on-the-scene assistance), others by a very capable caterer and staff.

The first year of our attendance I slipped behind the bar more to escape the mass of people (mingling and working the crowd is not one of my specialties) than to help the hired bartender…he was doing just fine. The next morning I said to Jack, "I know cutting the cost of your party isn't a primary goal, but maybe you don't need to employee a bartender. Dorothy and I can do it, since the skill of making mixed drinks isn't required" (available refreshments being soft drinks, bottled water, beer, and wine). So it has been since. We rather enjoyed the idea that the folks assume we are hired help, not clergy and spouse, until…the year I was privileged to conduct the marriage celebration at Second Presbyterian, Bloomington, for our friend's son and his bride. Many who attended the wedding also are invited to the Christmas party. That year some approached the bar with a quizzical expression. One gentleman finally asked the question that was apparently on the mind of some others: "I believe we've met before, but I regret I can't remember where." "It's likely it was here last Christmas," I offered. "No…somewhere else," he countered. When he returned, with his wife, for a third glass of chardonnay, he said, "Aren't you the Minister who officiated at Corey and Beth's wedding recently?" "That's right." "What are you doing behind the bar?!" his wife asked. "Trying to save Jack a few bucks." (They both work for Jack at upper management levels with State Farm, all receiving pretty decent financial remuneration!) "It feels funny having a clergy and his wife serve us drinks." They took their full glasses with them anyway.

Later in the evening, as the word circulated among some of the other guests, "That IS the Preacher behind the bar!" A debutant-type appeared at the corner of the bar. "What may I serve you?" I asked.
"Can we talk for a moment?" she wanted to know. "Certainly," I answered as I signaled Dorothy that the bar was all hers for awhile. "I've been wanting to ask my Pastor this, but am embarrassed to. You seem different…tending bar for goodness sake! What does the Bible say about…?" Quite an informal pastoral counseling session followed.

One never knows, as Christ's person – regardless of our varied roles in the Lord's ministries – when and how God will use us. Be prepared.

Ponderable

"You can live on bland food so as to avoid an ulcer, drink no tea, coffee or other stimulants in the name of health, go to bed early, stay away from night life, avoid all controversial subjects so as never to give offense, mind your own business, avoid involvement in other people's problems, spend money only on necessities, and save all you can. You can still break your neck in the bath tub, and it will serve you right." (Eileen Guder)

BUFFET

Do you not know that your body is a temple of the Holy Spirit within you, which you have from God? You are not your own; you were bought with a price. So glorify God in your body. (I Corinthians 6:19-20)

Prayer: *Send out Your light and Your truth, O God, that they may lead me, and bring me to Your holy hill, and to Your dwelling. Amen. (Psalm 63:3)*

ALL-YOU-CAN-EAT BUFFET

Why stop when you're full?! Two-thirds of Americans are overweight, regardless of whose charts are used, and regardless of my old excuses: I'm big boned….I may have a glandular problem….My metabolism rate is very low. Child obesity has reached threatening heights. By most votes, Mario Battalia is the nation's favorite, most successful TV chef/entrepreneur. Little wonder. His girth, we pretend, justifies our fatness.

I was particularly eager to have a look at Gatlinburg because I had read about it in a wonderful book called The Lost Continent. In it the author describes the scene on Main Street thusly: "Walking in an unhurried fashion up and down the street were more crowds of overweight tourists in boisterous clothes, with cameras bouncing on their bellies, consuming ice creams, cotton candy and corndogs, sometimes simultaneously." And so it was today. The same throngs of pear-shaped people in Reeboks wandered between food smells, clutching grotesque food and bucket-sized soft drinks. It is still the same tacky, horrible place." (Bill Bryson, A Walk in the Woods)

We all know there are other options. What some of us may not know, or ignore, is the command to glorify God in our bodies.

Fast food places also offer salads. Ordering half-portions or sharing a meal at restaurants is acceptable (they are glad for our business) and wise. Lo-cal, low-carb does not automatically translate into "tasteless"….Be creative with spices and herbs. Have you tried freshly squeezed lemon juice on your mixed greens instead of a sugar-laden salad dressing? When is the last time you compared the calories in a regular soft drink with a "diet" one – it takes only two cans to get used to the change in taste. Vegetarian…skim milk…stone ground wheat…reduced fat cheese. You already know all this and more, don't you? Are you ready, with God's help, to translate knowing into believing so that it becomes doing?

Moderate exercise, thirty minutes, five days a week, for those of us who are not preparing for a triathlon. No more tobacco – helpful medication is available. Eliminate alcohol Monday through Friday; enjoy in moderation on weekends (red wine has the least sugar). Goal: One day at a time (Alcoholics Anonymous proves it can work). Diet plans abound (I favor The South Beach Diet); note the small print on most TV and magazine ads offering testimonies like, "I lost 80 pounds in four months" (small print: Not Typical Results). Replace "I hate depriving myself like this!" with, "I'm gifting myself and my loved ones with a healthier, happier me"…. and pleasing God.

Here's the one Dorothy models for me: Stop eating when you're full! Not everything on the buffet needs to be consumed. Your mother's "Clean your plate; there are starving children in China who would love to have that food" becomes a grownup, "I'll eat it all; I just won't fill the plate full."

The Lord's power to you.

Ponderable

"Primary health issues in the 1980's were lifestyle-related: heart disease and hypertension related to stress, cancers associated with a toxic environment, AIDS contracted through drug use and sexual activity, sexually transmitted diseases, emphysema and lung cancer caused by cigarette smoking, fetal damage resulting from maternal alcohol and drug abuse, diabetes and other diet-related disorders, violent crime, automobile accidents involving alcohol.

These were concerns for health experts in the United States in the 1980's and nothing has altered the trend since then. Studies at the Jimmy Carter Center in Atlanta show that two-thirds of deaths prior to age sixty-five can be traced to behavioral choices.

Having spent much of his working life in India, Dr. Paul Brand had attended comparable medical conferences there. In India, he told me, our top ten health concerns would consist of infectious diseases: malaria, polio, dysentery, tuberculosis, typhoid fever, leprosy. If you promised Indian health experts the eradication of their top ten diseases, they could hardly imagine such a paradise. Yet look what has happened in America. After conquering most of those infectious diseases, the U.S. has now substituted new health problems for old, the majority of them stemming from lifestyle choices.

Dr. Brand recalled a U.S. health meeting that was held in Arizona. That state's neighbor to the west, Nevada, ranks as the very worst on most mortality tables, while its northern neighbor, Utah, ranks as the best. Both states have a relatively wealthy and well-educated population, and they share a similar climate. The difference in health is best explained by lifestyle factors. Utah is the seat of Mormonism, which frowns on alcohol, tobacco, and caffeine. Nevada has twice the incidence of divorce and a far higher rate of alcohol and tobacco use, not to mention the unique stress associated with gambling."
(Philip Yancey, Rumors of Another World, 2003)

SONGS

Remember what Christ taught, and let His words enrich your lives and make you wise; teach them to each other, and sing them out in psalms and hymns and spiritual songs, singing them to the Lord with thankful hearts.

(Colossians 3:16)

Prayer: *Bless to me, O God, each thing mine eye sees; bless to me, O God, each sound mine ear hears; bless to me, O God, each odor that goes to my nostrils; bless to me, O God, each taste that goes to my lips. Amen. (The Celtic Way of Prayer)*

An article appearing in Journal for Preachers (Pentecost, 2006) titled "God's Good Gift," has John L. Bell of Scotland's Iona Community offering this "throw away" sentence: "When it comes to Jesus' enjoying food and drink, a constant in the Gospels, nothing is celebrated in song."

Can you think of a hymn, praise or gospel song, anthem – any piece of secular or sacred music with reference to what clearly is a constant Gospel Truth: the Lord delighted in food and beverage? I can't. Neither can Jason Montague, McDonough Presbyterian's outstanding Director of Music who is as knowledgeable as they come.   His wife, Araminta, who does astonishing things with our Children's Choir and Children's Handchime Choir, couldn't think of one either. Jane Robinson, our talented and equally knowledgeable Church Musician, came up empty handed as well. Ditto Wes Shannon, our skilled Adult Choir accompanist. I feel obliged to try,

Wining and dining the Master came; Jesus' enemies said, "It's a terrible shame. The Baptizer's boys fast in proper form, but Your guys all break the norm."

"God's Party has begun!", insisted the Son; "Strike up the band, upgrade the bland; Messiah's Banquet will be quite grand. All are invited, none will banned!"

OK, so I'm not a song writer! See what you can do.

Ponderable

"The statistics are clear: kids who dine with their families are healthier, happier and better students, which is why a dying tradition is coming back." (Nancy Gibbs, "The Magic of the Family Meal," Time, June 12, 2006)

Entrée

Arroz Con Pollo

2 (5 oz.) packages Vigo yellow rice
1 large sweet onion
4 oz. jar of sliced pimento
1 cup green olives stuffed with pimento
8 oz. frozen baby green peas
2 boneless/skinless chicken breasts
Olive oil or butter
Garlic powder

Pound thawed chicken breasts to a more uniform thickness; cut each breast into 4 chunks. Brown chicken in olive oil or butter in medium-hot skillet no more than 15 minutes, turning often enough to keep from overbrowning. Sprinkle both sides lightly with garlic powder. Set chicken aside.

Prepare rice per package instructions. When water with the rice reaches a boil, put in the chicken pieces and reduce heat to low. After 25 minutes, check rice for tenderness and to see if all the water has been absorbed. When rice is done, fluff with a large fork. While rice is cooking, dice the onion into a separate pot with 1/2 cup of water and a teaspoon of olive oil or butter and a shake of garlic powder. When the water is boiling, add the frozen peas and cook according to package directions. When the peas and onion mixture, as well as the rice with chicken, are done, add them together. Then add the olives and pimento, mixing well with a large spoon.

Yield: 4 servings

(Phil Bowden)

Dressing

Dijon Vinaigrette

2 T. balsamic vinegar
2 T. coarse-grain Dijon mustard
¼ t. sugar
¼ cup olive oil

Whisk together first 3 ingredients in a small bowl; gradually whisk in olive oil.

(Aubrey Robinson)

Vegetable

Brussels Sprouts with Crisp Prosciutto

3 cups trimmed and halved Brussels sprouts (1-1/2 pounds)
1/4 cup chopped prosciutto (1-1/2 oz.)
Cooking spray
1 tablespoon butter
1/2 teaspoon salt
1/4 teaspoon black pepper
1 tablespoon fresh lemon juice

Cook Brussels sprouts in boiling water until done, about 5 minutes; drain. Heat a large nonstick skillet over medium heat; add prosciutto. Cook 6 minutes or until crisp, stirring occasionally. Remove from pan and set aside. Heat pan coated with cooking spray over medium-high heat. Add sprouts and sauté for at least 3 minutes or until lightly brown. Add butter, salt, and pepper, stirring until butter melts. Remove from heat, drizzle with juice. Add prosciutto and toss to combine.

Yield: 6 servings

(Dorothy Rose)

MARKET

And His gifts were that some should be apostles, some prophets, some evangelists, some pastors and teachers, to equip the saints for the work of ministry, for building up the body of Christ....(Ephesians 4:11-12)

Prayer: *Grant me on earth what seems Thee best, 'till death and Heav'n reveal the rest. Amen. (Isaac Watts)*

Whole Foods Market, Inc., has much about it to admire. When Mrs. Rose decides our family food budget can tolerate their pricey (nickname: Whole Paycheck) products, I grocery shop at their market on Atlanta's Ponce de Leon Avenue. Their quality and variety, combined with the manner in which the goods are displayed, are admirable. As is the fact that, since 1998, Whole Foods has ranked high among Fortune's "100 Best Companies to Work for in America." In 2004, according to Financial Times, Whole Foods was "the fastest-growing mass retailer in the U.S." I also admire their policy of limiting the compensation of their highest-paid executives to no more than fourteen times the employee salary average.

John Mackey, founder and C.E.O. of Whole Foods, once told Forbes,

> Business is simple. Management's job is to take care of employees. The employee's
> job is to take care of the customers. Happy customers take care of the shareholders.
> (All of the above from Steven Shapin, "Paradise Sold," The New Yorker, May 15, 2006)

I'm not a fan of business models becoming the Church's guide for carrying out our Christ-appointed ministries. While we are, in part, a human institution with budgets and employees, Jesus' Church, as you know, is not to be about profit and loss, time studies to improve productivity, inflexible personnel manuals complete with dress codes, et. al. Sure, we have bills and salaries to pay, accountability to each other to honor, guidelines for tasks, and behavior to note. But our calling as God's people known as the Body of Christ on earth, is less to be successful by secular standards and more to be faithful by our Lord's criterion.

Yet, might there be a mini-lesson from Whole Foods for us in the Church to consider? An equitable balance in compensation for a church's professional and support staffs...spiritual leaders taking care of one another and those employees with whom we labor, toward the goal of all of us taking care of the customers (congregation)...thereby yielding a happy congregation that takes better care of the Church's only shareholder, Jesus.

Steven Shapin again,

> I like to shop at Whole Foods. Sometimes I go there just to see the variety and the
> colors: what new kinds of chard and kale will they have today? The employees –
> "team members" as they're called – seem reasonably happy and are often quite
> knowledgeable about the things they sell.

I have no reservations about applying that image to the Church:
variety and colors: country club members and their caddies/kitchen help…apartments and condos and trailer parks and high-rent district residents…singled and coupled…employee and employer and unemployed…tan and white and black…southern brogued, New England clipped, Jamican lilted;
team members: reasonably happy to represent God's people in the community, speaking a good word (by deed and voice) where we live and move and have our being…well coached and prepared to play the game…knowledgeable about God's game plan for the Church (although we believe we have nothing to sell – God's love in Christ is a gift).

A new view of whole food: whole as complete; food as Jesus, the Bread of Life. May God grow Jesus' Church by the Spirit's power, profiting us and others with Gospel blessings and responsibilities.

Ponderable

"Jesus commissions the Twelve to feed His hungry sheep, all five thousand of them, with five loaves, two sardines. 'You give them something to eat.' (Mark 6:37) The disciples don't get it. Most days neither do I. Like the disciples in Mark, I tend to think ministry is about me. Even after all these years, that's the trap I still spring on myself. It's about my ability to pull it off – whatever it is. The feeding of the multitude by Jesus' disciples should forever have laid that bird to rest. The disciples don't do a thing but deliver to others what Jesus has already blessed and broken and given to God. All are fed and satisfied. They even have leftovers, all because the little they have is offered to God and blessed by Jesus. He is the chef; we're not. We're the Domino's pizza couriers – no more, but certainly no less."

©. Clifton Black, Professor, Princeton Theological Seminary, in a sermon preached
June 24, 2005 at the Seminary's Miller Chapel and published in The Princeton Seminary Bulletin)

BETRAYAL

During supper (the Feast of the Passover), when the devil had already put it into the heart of Judas Iscariot to betray Jesus....(John 13:2)

Prayer: *Our Father, bless us as we eat; let love make every morsel sweet. We thank Thee for Thy gifts this day. May all our needs be met, we pray. Amen.*

(Stuart R. Oglesby, Prayers for All Occasions, 1940)

Judas' betrayal (blame it on "the devil made me do it" or not), must have made for, to put it mildly, an uncomfortable meal time. Can you imagine what it felt like around the room that evening? I'm not so sure I can. But Jesus knew. Judas knew. Very soon the eleven would know. After the foot washing the Messiah would tell them, "Truly, truly, I say to you, one of you will betray me."

What sadness for all, but especially for Jesus. His last meal with these fellows, and the Passover Feast yet. Talk about spoiling a dinner party!

Fred and Nettie Craddock experienced a much milder version of having a damper put on a party.

> Last fall my wife, Nettie, and I attended a victory party following a University of Georgia football game. We didn't know anybody there except the couple with whom we were in attendance. It was held in a marvelous home in a suburb of Atlanta – Victorian, restored, beautiful, high ceilings, well appointed, and expensive. A lot of people were there, maybe thirty, thirty-five people, mostly in their forties and early fifties. They were dressed up in the kind of clothing that says, "How 'Bout Them Dawgs." It was quite an exciting thing. We emptied the cars, went inside, and put away the coats. The host and hostess put out those little sandwiches and the drink, and then the talk began, introducing each other around to make sure we all knew each other. There was an attractive woman there, I don't know her name, a little too bejeweled and overdressed to have just come from a ball game, just dripping with success, as was her husband and all the people there, and she stood up in front of all of us while we were getting into the party and said, "I think we ought to sing the Doxology."

> Before we could even vote on it, she started. She and few others sang with gusto. Some stood there and counted their shoelaces, some tried to find a place to set their drinks down because you shouldn't hold one during the Doxology. There were a few that hummed along, like I did. I was sort of in between there; I confess to feeling a bit awkward.

> When we finished singing the Doxology, this beautiful woman said, mostly to the men, "You can talk all you want about the running of Herschel Walker, but it was Jesus that gave us the victory." Somebody said, "You really believe that?" She said, "Of course I do. Jesus said, 'Whatever you ask, ask for in my name,' and He'll give it to you. So I said, 'Jesus, I want us to win more than anything in the world,' and we won. I'm not ashamed to say that it's because of Jesus, because I'm not ashamed of the gospel."

Some of us were beginning to move to other parts of the house. I walked over toward the kitchen; it was kind of awkward. Most of the people were beginning to go silent, and she said, "I'm not ashamed to just say it anywhere, because Jesus told us to shout it from the housetops." I'm already in the kitchen and I can hear it. Some of us were standing in the kitchen, trying to get into some of the details and relive the game that had just been played, when the hostess came into the kitchen. There was a silence when she came in, during which one of the men said to me, "Do you think that woman's drunk?" I said, "Well, I don't know. We just moved to Georgia last year." I mean, I was glad that Georgia won, but I was not feverish about it. As the hostess went about refilling her tray with little sandwiches, she said, if I may quote her, "If she doesn't shut her damn mouth, she's going to ruin my party."

(Craddock Stories, edited by Mike Graves and Richard F. Ward, 2001)

Amplify that awkward situation to the nth degree and it may approach the level of tension so long ago in the Upper Room.

Do you think Jesus considered bailing out that evening? I would have been tempted to. I mean, three years with this group of intimate friends, and still a turncoat? It may be that Jesus hung in by adopting – originating, really – one of the mantras of the students of group process (a Doctor of Ministry course I took, officially called Ministry With Groups, at Chicago's McCormick Theological Seminary with Professor Hugh Halverstadt): There are times when we do well to lose an individual in order to save the group…Groups supercede individuals, so never allow one person to destroy a group. Regrettably, once, I had to resort to such an unpleasant responsibility, with a Session member.

The hostess at Georgia's victory party might have tried it, too: Please put an end to your high- pressure evangelizing at my party; you're spoiling the evening for my other guests. If you won't, I'll show you the front door…and then we'll discuss it all over coffee and croissants in the morning. Note, please, that Jesus sent Judas on his way that night (What you are going to do, Judas, do quickly) but did not send him away without another opportunity to repair their relationship: As Judas led the SWAT team to arrest Jesus in Gethsemane, planting his betrayal kiss on the Lord's cheek, Jesus responded, "Friend…." (Matthew 26:50) The door was still open.

Parties aren't just about you. Behave yourself…and try not to burn bridges.

Ponderable

> Not passive. Not aggressive. Assertive.

FRIENDS

There are friends who pretend to be friends, but there is a friend who sticks closer than a brother.

(Proverbs 18:24)

Julius treated Paul kindly, and gave him leave to go to his friends and be cared for.

(Acts 27:3)

Prayer: *Our Father, we thank Thee for those who have helped us along life's journey, who have cheered and inspired us and looked for the good in us that was often not immediately apparent. May we never withhold our help from those who are struggling and discouraged. As Thou hast blessed us so greatly, grant that we may continually strive to be a great blessing to our fellow men. In Jesus' name. Amen. (Stuart R. Oglesby, Prayers for All Occasions, 1940)*

It's not clear to me whether Proverbs intends to make a point by noting a distinction between friends and a friend, but that's how I read it: living brings a bunch of friends to us, some of them pretending to be friends…and others offering the rare gift, a friend who sticks close.

St. Paul, like us, knew both…friends who were similar to shadows (they disappear as soon as the sun isn't shining in our lives or theirs – fair weather friends) and a friend or two who are closer even than those with blood ties. Think of the apostle, from his Roman prison cell, writing,

> Demas has deserted me, Crescens is off in Galatia, Titus to Dalmatia…Alexander
> the coppersmith did me great harm…but Luke is with me now…bring Mark along
> with you, Timothy, when you come…and greet Prisca, Aquila, Onesiphorus' family…
> hurry to me, Timothy, my son in the faith, my beloved child.
> (II Timothy 1:2; 4:9-22)

Friends who pretend to be friends – Demas, etc., and a friend who sticks closer than a brother – Luke, Mark, Timothy.

The context of Acts 27:3 is that Paul, having survived an assassination attempt, once more is a prisoner of Rome, having been accused by some Jewish leaders of blasphemy. In a complicated case of law (aren't most of them!?), the Pharisaical-Jew-now-turned-Jesus'-man is shipped off to Italy to be dealt with, at his own insistence, by no less than Caesar himself. As Paul and other prisoners sail, a stop for supplies at the port city of Sidon is commanded, and that brings us to our text,

Julius (guard in command of the chain gang), treated Paul kindly and gave him leave (a one day prison pass, a brief parole) to go to his friends and be cared for.

I'm as sure as I can be that the caring by those genuine friends included providing their finest comfort foods. I would have prepared Paul some of my Italian wedding soup. Buddy Welch would have slowly cooked collard greens. Aubrey Robinson would have gotten out the chilled buttermilk into which cornbread could be dipped. Jean Foster's chocolate cheesecake would be served. Jack North would mix a perfect dry martini (olive, not onion). Please now add your own favorite comfort food: _____.

If Gayden Metcalfe and Charlotte Hays were involved, the comfort food would be headed by tomato aspic. From their book, Being Dead Is No Excuse – The Official Southern Ladies Guide to Hosting the Perfect Funeral (2005)...

> Can you be buried without tomato aspic? Not in the Mississippi Delta, you can't.
> We've never been to a funeral where homemade aspic wasn't served. Store-bought
> aspic is available, but no self-respecting Southerner would be caught eating it. It is equally
> delicious with just mayonnaise, or with pickled shrimp, avocado slices, and other trimmings.

Here are a few more observations from the book. Enjoy chuckling!

> People in the Delta look better dead, whether in their coffins or obituaries. Although
> we sometimes succumb to the temptation to speak ill of the dead – usually in the
> car on the way from the cemetery to the house – we don't believe you have to have
> won a Nobel Prize to get a good obituary. A glowing obituary is practically a birthright
> in the Delta, and it should be a write-up that would not only please the deceased but
> gratify those left behind. Usually it does. Whatever you think about the purpose of
> the funeral , the obituary is for the living – at least, in the Delta, it is….

> While eulogists are going on and on during the funeral service about what a model
> citizen and devoted husband Mr. So-and-So was, we're trying to keep straight faces.
> He was a notorious fanny pincher and crook who was lucky not to have ended up behind
> bars. Yes, dead or alive, we'd all like to have praise heaped up on. But isn't it safer,
> really, to wait until everybody is at home with a toddy? That way, if you can't stop
> laughing, you can claim you had too much to drink….

> We'd better warn you not to put too much credence in the dates carved on the
> headstones. We Southern women tend to lie about our age – even when we're
> dead. Allison Parker, who always had a thing for younger men, made a complete
> fool of herself by knocking off five years. We died laughing when we saw the
> stone, because, if anybody looked her age, it was Allison Parker.

May Jesus, life's finest Friend to all who trust John 15:14, "You are my friends, if you do what I command you," bless you with a host of friends who stick closer than a blood relative…who care for you. And may you, by the power of God's Spirit, be such a friend.

Ponderable

"Our Father, we thank Thee for friends who believe in us and pray for us – friends whose faith in us make us better than we otherwise would be. We rejoice in all the opportunities that come to us for showing Christian friendship. Put it into our hearts to make one of the most earnest efforts of our Christian lives that of being friends to those in need, and better friends to those whose lives we touch in Christian service. For Jesus' sake. Amen." (Stuart R. Oglesby, Prayers for All Occasions, 1940)

Soup

Italian Wedding Soup

1 large whole chicken (at least three pounds)
2 pounds ground beef
2 eggs
4 cloves minced garlic
¼ cup parmesan cheese
Hot sauce
Italian bread crumbs
Chicken broth
2 large onions
4-6 stalks celery, diced
Garlic salt
1 bag spinach or endive

Fill large pot 2/3 full. Half should be water and other half chicken broth. Add 2 diced onions, diced celery, garlic salt, salt, and pepper. Wash chicken and add, cooking at a slow boil until it "falls apart" (about 1 hour). While chicken is cooking, make meatballs. Combine ground beef, eggs, garlic, parmesan cheese, hot sauce, salt, and pepper. Add breadcrumbs until meat can be rolled into very small meatballs. Brown in medium hot skillet with a touch of oil. Drain well. Remove chicken from pot and let cool. Put meatballs into water and chicken broth mixture. As they cook, the meatballs will float to the top. Pull meat from chicken, discarding, skin, etc., and cut into small pieces. Add to broth and meatballs. Add spinach or endive to pot, pushing it down as you cook. It will shrink in time, so use your own judgment as to how much you would like. Let cook "all day" on low heat. Skim fat from surface and season to taste. Top each bowl with parmesan cheese.

(Gloria Florie)

Vegetable

Roasted Leeks

6 small leeks
1 to 2 T. olive oil
1/4 t. salt
1/4 t. pepper
1/2 t. chopped fresh thyme

Remove root, tough outer leaves, and tops from leeks, leaving 2 inches of dark leaves. Cut in half lengthwise; rinse well and drain. Stir together the remaining ingredients; toss with leeks. Place cut side down on lightly greased jellyroll pan. Bake at 450°F for 25 minutes or until lightly brown and wilted. Serve with Dijon vinaigrette. Serves 6.

(Aubrey Robinson)

Dessert

Key Lime Cake

3/4 cup orange juice
1-1/3 cups oil
5 eggs
1 box lemon cake mix
1 small package lime Jell-o gelatin
1/3 cup Key lime juice
4 T. powdered sugar
1 stick butter
8 oz. package cream cheese
1 lb. box powdered sugar
3/4 cup pecans, chopped
1 t. vanilla

Mix the juice, oil, eggs, cake mix and lime Jell-o for the cake batter. Grease and flour three 9-inch cake pans and pour batter into pans. Bake at 350°F degrees for 25 minutes. While cake bakes, mix lime juice and 4 T. powdered sugar together for glaze. Cool cake completely on racks. For icing, mix the butter and cream cheese. Add box of powdered sugar gradually. Beat until smooth. Add vanilla and nuts. Ice each layer, but brush each layer with glaze before icing.

(Jeanne Christie)

LUNCH

In the morning, as Jesus was returning to Jerusalem, He was hungry, and noticed a fig tree beside the road.

(Matthew 21:18)

Morning Prayer: *As the day's light breaks the darkness of the night, as the first movements of the morning pierce the night's stillness, so a new waking to life dawns in me, so a fresh beginning opens. In the early light of this day, in the first actions of the morning, let me be awake to life. In my soul and in my seeing, let me be alive to the gift of this new day; let me be fully alive. (J. Philip Newell, Sounds of the Eternal, A Celtic Psalter)*

Steven Shapin is quoting Gene Kahn in a The New Yorker (May 15, 2006) article about pros and cons of organic farming. Gene was the founder of Washington State's Cascadian Farm and recently sold a majority holding to Welch's (now a division of the food giant, General Mills). A "onetime hippie," Gene is critical of what he thinks is too much hype about the blessings of organically grown products.

On the place that food has in the average person's life, Mr. Kahn insists,

"This is just lunch for most people. Just lunch. We can call it sacred,
we can talk about communion, but it's just lunch."

I had about two-thirds of this book's chapters completed when I read the above. Maybe he is right, I thought. Am I overstating my theme? I have no qualms about Life Lessons From the Table, believing the Bible is full of spiritual truths revolving around food and eating. Jesus, for instance, made quite a Divine Truth out of the withering of the fig tree (Matthew 21:18-22). I doubt we should read it as just an early lunch. Yet, Gene Kahn's "This is just lunch" may well be a corrective to any of my book's possible exaggerations. You be the judge.

Footnote. The Roses joined the Albrights in September, 2006, splurging at Atlanta's five-star Seegers Restaurant. Splendid in every way. Departing, I picked up a complimentary book, Les Grandes Tables du Monde, Traditions and Qualite, 2006. For more than fifty years it has been listing what they believe are the most prestigious restaurants all over the world. Extreme exaggerations abound!

For instance, this restaurant (La Tour d' Argent, Paris) will make your meal an "interval from the absurd, and a stolen moment away from the everyday gloom." Dorothy doesn't think I've overstated my case, but my wife is a bit prejudiced in my favor! The secretary in a middle school counselor's office, Mrs. Rose illustrated her agreement with my book's theme: Almost every day, the Union Grove Middle School counselors and staff gather around a table in their office for lunch. "We've never set any rules about it," Dorothy said, "but no one begins eating until all of us are present. That may not be a big deal to some, but I think it says something important about why we all get along so well in often stressful working conditions. We smiled at each other a couple days ago when a seventh-grade teacher walked by our table and said, 'You all seem to have such a good time together!' We know enjoying lunch together is one reason why."

On the place food has in the average person's life: "This is just lunch for most people." Maybe Gene…only maybe.

Ponderable

Because of an editing error, a recipe last Wednesday for meatballs with an article about foods to serve during the Super Bowl misstated the amount of chipotle chilies in adobo to be used. It is one or two canned chilies, not one or two cans. (From The New York Times)

ROOKIE
Hebrews 5:11-14

Prayer: *O God, You have set before us a great hope that Your Kingdom will come on earth, and have taught us to pray for its coming: make us ready to thank You for the signs of its dawning, and to pray and work for the perfect day when Your will shall be done on earth as it is in heaven. In the name of Jesus Christ. Amen. (Iona Abbey Worship Book, Scotland's Iona Community, 2001)*

Lessons I did not learn in the kindergarten of cooking, but wish I had: Sharpen knife before every use; Lemon juice removes most kitchen odors from the hands; Save the asparagus stocks for making soup (freeze until a sufficient quantity is accumulated); Using a blender beats whisking; Containers of 99% fat-free chicken or beef broth are nearly as good as the time-consuming homemade kind; Frozen diced vegetables work just fine (especially the onions); Don't hang garlic in the light – it's in the lily family, so treat it as you would any bulb: keep in a cool, dark place; Kosher and/or sea salt and fresh ground black or white pepper are a must; Heat skillet before adding oil; Turn meat, et. al., as infrequently as possible (I used to fiddle with it constantly, losing juices); Tuck your fingers in (knuckles-only showing) while holding product you're slicing; Be especially careful of the mandolin (I'll show you my scarred finger tip); A damp towel under the plastic cutting board keeps it from slipping; Eighteen seconds on high in the microwave will wilt spinach/greens nicely and with less effort than sautéing them.

Lessons, after nearly twenty years at the range and cutting board, I'm still trying to learn: how to crack an egg with one hand; the art of turning food in a skillet by flipping rather than stirring (I practiced for a while with dried beans in the pan – to no avail); how to slice and then cut an onion so it is diced neatly and quickly (the TV chefs make it appear quite easy); how to cut with a rocking rather than slicing motion.

By the way, chop, dice, and mince – what they are and how they differ can be confusing. So here's a quick guide to help you: For chopped food, think of gambling dice, roughly 5/8" x 5/8". It's a good cut to use when making dishes that cook awhile, such as stews, soups and stocks. When dicing, keep a pencil eraser in mind, 1/4 – 3/8" x 1/4 – 3/8". If something has to be sautéed for short periods of time or eaten raw, as in salsa, then dice it. Mincing is just cutting food into tiny bits. When you mince garlic or shallots, the small pieces spread throughout a dish, permeating it with flavor. To mince, first roughly chop or dice the food, then rock your knife back and forth over it until it's small.

Rookies in all areas of life do well to pay attention in the minor leagues. Let the pros who coach you pass on their wisdom (…remember Crash Davis, the pro catcher, and Nuke LaRoche, the rookie pitcher, in the movie, Bull Durham?). Learn as a kindergartner-rookie to cook from the Ph.D's: Emeril and Sarah and Rachael and Mario and Mom and Dad and Grandma and spouse and friend.

Rookies, even when they reach the big leagues (Crash called it "the show"), know they are still learning. New recipes and old cookbooks combine in the life of a grown-up cook. There remain challenges at the range and oven that can feel as daunting as ones we experienced in kindergarten (Creme Brulee, water bath or not, is still on my list). To hang it all up and leave the cooking to someone else is tempting some days: Dorothy arrived home just in time to retrieve a bunch of asparagus tips from the wastebasket and suggested kindly that they, not the stalks I had in the pan, were to be steamed. Feeling quite silly, I wondered if I had better find a new hobby.

Have you seen lately a TV rerun of A League of Their Own, the nearly true story of our country's first professional women's softball team? Tom Hanks is the hard-drinking coach. Geena Davis is the "star" player.

Discouraged, for a good many reasons, she tells the coach,

> "This is too hard. I quit. I'm going home."

Hanks' response,

> "Of course it's hard. If it were easy, everyone would do it."

Following Jesus is hard, too. Moving from spiritual milk to spiritual solid food (I Corinthians 3:2) is hard. Transitioning from Jesus' rookie to Christ's grown-up disciple is hard. Kindergarten to grad school with the Master is hard. If it were easy, everyone would do it.

Ponderable

Quit and go home, or hang in/hang on until, with St. Paul, we can affirm, "I have fought the good fight; I have finished the race; I have kept the faith." (II Timothy 4:7)

MEATBALLS

Jesus, A friend of tax collectors and sinners. (Matthew 11:19b)

Prayer: *God, I'm trying to get up this mountain, but every time I get near the top, I get knocked down again. I'm not asking You to get me all the way to the peak, but could You hold my hand, and, please, not let me fall any further into the abyss? (Rabbi Hirshel Jaffe)*

It was a clandestine affair. Six men on a Saturday morning locked in the kitchen of the church I was serving, making meatballs. The time and place had been chosen to assure as much privacy as possible, and because of the powerful exhaust fan that would, we hoped, suck away the smoke from our Winstons and Marlboros. Locked doors were due to the adequate supply of Stroh's beer in the large cooler, hardly appropriate for a church kitchen.

It was not ground chuck we used, sadly, but the fatty stuff…let alone doing it right by mixing in some veal. The other five "cooks" were full blooded Italians, requiring more garlic than this WASP deemed necessary. The concept of making our own, as I do now, bread crumbs never crossed our minds. It seemed to me, as well, that the amount of ketchup poured in was over the top.

The meatballs were to join spaghetti, Italian bread and salad at a fund raiser that night at the Koppel (PA) Fire Station, benefiting the Riverside High School football program where we coached. A team, I'm proud to announce – as attested by knowledgeable fans and rival coaches – who won more games, in my nine years on the coaching staff, with less talented players than any other local team. I would not mislead you. We had a few exceptionally gifted athletes who earned football scholarships to Division I universities (like Pitt, Miami, Louisville, Kentucky, and Indiana) and Division II colleges (Toledo, Mt. Union, and Appalachian State), but the heart of the squads was formed by pretty ordinary guys who were extraordinarily coached. Credit Head Coach Karl Florie. We earned the Western Pennsylvania IIA Championship in 1985 with a mere thirty-three players on the roster.

No meatballs and spaghetti meal has ever tasted as good to me as the one served in an honest-to-God hole-in-the-wall (a steelmill worker's shot-and-beer bar at one end and a dozen tables at the other, separated by the messiest one commode-restroom ever found in a public place): The Corner Tavern, Beaver Falls, PA. You may know Beaver Falls High as home to Alabama's/New York Jet's Joe Namath, against whom I played.

I realized while coaching, and remember with fondness now, how helpful it was for Dorothy and me to have, for the first time, a circle of friends outside of the Church I served…especially friends with whom we, on the surface, had little in common. As mentioned, the coaching staff were mostly Italian; all Roman Catholic; many used to a different lifestyle (You don't smoke and drink in the church kitchen in my circle!); small town, second-and third-generation families. No negative reflection on Church friends should be deduced. It's just that without Karl, Ronnie, Pete, Raymond, Sam, Bobby, and Chuck in the coaches' room and at coaches' family gatherings, I would have missed so much: bocce games at the Italian Mutual Benefit Society Club (where, as far as I know, I still am the only non-Italian to be granted an honorary membership); coaches' convention in Pittsburgh with the big names of the day lecturing (and watching, from the sidelines, high stake poker games – I stuck with Liar's Poker); nights scouting and mornings grading film; parties after victories, pep rallies, arguing with each other about whether the quarterback draw or quick pitch or belly series or stop-and-go pass would work best against such-and-such defense; practice on frozen turf Thanksgiving morning preparing for a weekend playoff game; having my nose broken while quarterbacking our "get ready" team (the second stringers who ran next week's opponent's plays against our defense squad); KDKA TV, Pittsburgh, doing a half-hour documentary on me, "The Clergy Coach"; and, hopefully, the privilege of influencing the lives of some teenage boys through the game of football. (It pleased me that my first year the team captains announced I would be addressed as "Rev" rather than "Coach," honoring my calling as a minister.)

It would be a ridiculous stretch to propose that my football friendships were justified by Jesus' seeming to feel more at home with "tax collectors and sinners" than He did the "church" of His day. But it's not a stretch to maintain that my life is richer because of those years as part of The Riverside Football Panther Family.

I rarely make meatballs – like the tiny ones that are an integral part of Italian Wedding Soup (see recipe included) – without a smile and a "thank you, Karl, and the guys."

Have you considered opening yourself to some folks a bit different than your usual crowd… perhaps not "your own kind"…widening your circle? I'm glad I did.

P.S. Karl was inducted into the prestigious Pennsylvania High School Football Coaches Hall of Fame in 2006. A most deserved honor.

Ponderable

My favorite part of two-a-day practices was Biff's daily talks about Building Men for Others. Prior to afternoon practices, the boys streamed into the meticulously maintained field house. The talks usually lasted twenty to thirty minutes. "I expect greatness out of you," the coach told the boys. "And the way we measure greatness is the impact you make on other people's lives." How would the boys make the most impact? For one thing, they would make an impact by being inclusive rather than exclusive. "The rest of the world will always try to separate you," Biff said. "That's almost a law of nature, gonna happen no matter what, right? The rest of the world will want to separate you by race, by socio-economic status, by education levels, by religion, by neighborhood, by what kind of car you drive, by the clothes you wear, by athletic ability. You name it – always gonna be people who want to separate by that stuff. Well, if you let that happen now, then you'll let it happen later. Don't let it happen. If you're one of us, part of this football team, then you won't walk around putting people into pigeonholes. Not now. Not ever. Because every single one of them has something to offer. Every single one of them is special. We are a program of inclusion," Biff said. "We do not believe in separation." The boys would also make an impact by breaking down cliques and stereotypes, by developing empathy and kindness for all. "If you can put yourself in another man's shoes, that's a great gift to have for a lifetime." That was the whole idea behind the ironclad rule that no Gilman High School football player should ever let another Gilman boy – teammate or not – eat lunch by himself. "You happen to see another boy off by himself, go sit with him or bring him over to sit with you and your friends," Biff said. "I don't care if you know him or not. I don't care if he's the best athlete in the school or the so-called nerd with his head always down in the books. You go get him and you make him feel wanted."
(Jeffrey Marx, Seasons of Life, 2003)

Entrée

Lasagna Rolls

1 package lasagna strips
1 egg, beaten
1 pound ricotta cheese
8 oz. mozzarella
2 tablespoons salad oil
2 medium onions, chopped
2 large garlic cloves, minced
1-1/2 pounds lean ground beef
1 cup parsley, chopped
1 teaspoon basil
1/4 teaspoon salt
1/2 teaspoon oregano
1/4 teaspoon pepper
31 oz. spaghetti sauce

White Sauce

2 tablespoons butter
2 tablespoons flour
1-1/2 cups milk
1 cup Parmesan cheese
1/2 teaspoon salt
1/4 teaspoon pepper

Add lasagna noodles to boiling water and cook 10 minutes. Drain in cold water. Lay strips side-by-side on towels. Prepare filling in a large bowl. Combine beaten egg, ricotta, and mozzarella. Set aside. In large skillet, heat oil and sauté onions and garlic. Add beef and cook; drain off fat. Stir in parsley, basil, salt, oregano, and pepper. Let cool for a few minutes. Add beef mixture to the cheese mixture and blend together. Pour 3/4 jar of spaghetti sauce into bottom of 3-quart oblong pan. Spread each lasagna strip with about 1/4 cup of beef/cheese mixture then roll up jelly roll fashion. Put standing up in pan.
Prepare white sauce. Melt butter, stir in flour, gradually add milk. Cook and stir until mixture boils and thickens. Stir in Parmesan, salt, and pepper. Pour over rolls. Pour remaining spaghetti sauce over white sauce. Sprinkle with more Parmesan, if desired. Cover with foil and bake for 20 minutes at 400°F. Remove foil and bake 10 more minutes.

Yield: 18 servings
(Dorothy Rose)

Vegetable

Cold Marinated Green Beans

1¼ pounds green beans
3 T. red wine vinegar
1 T. Dijon mustard
¾ t. sugar
pepper
5 T. vegetable oil
¼ cup finely diced red onion
1T. minced dill

Cook beans; after boiling for 4 minutes, cool in ice to stop cooking. Drain. Whisk together vinegar, mustard, sugar, salt and pepper. Slowly add oil. Dressing will thicken. Just before serving, toss dressing, onion and dill with beans. Chill. Can be made the day ahead, but do not add dressing.

(Pat Robinson)

Soup

Cold Avocado Cucumber Soup

1 (10 ¾ oz.) can cream of celery soup
1 can water
1 cucumber, diced
1 avocado, peeled and diced
2 T. vegetable oil
½ green pepper, diced
3 green onions, chopped
1 medium tomato, diced
1 T. wine vinegar
salt and pepper to taste
garlic salt to taste
dill weed to taste

Combine all ingredients in bowl, mix well. Refrigerate and chill at least 1 hour. Serve topped with croutons, if desired.

(Kit Welch)

QUESTION

Have you any fish?   (John 21:5)
Have you anything to eat?   (Luke 24:41)

Prayer: *We do not ask so much for the strength which Thou hast promised, as for the grace to use what Thou hast already supplied in Christ Jesus, our Lord. Amen.*
(Paul Scherer, Love Is a Spendthrift, 1961)

Both questions come from the resurrected Lord. Both appear, in the Gospel writer's eyes, to have a practical purpose... although Jesus' inquiry from the beach to the unsuccessful fisherman disciples seems a rhetorical question: certainly, before asking, He knew the answer. St. John records the Christ once more startling His disciples back in Jerusalem, with a request for food (they gave Him a piece of boiled fish, not having a deep fryer available), so that the Risen One can demonstrate that He's not a spirit. Ghosts don't let you see them eat (verse 43). O ye of little faith.

There is more here, though, to our Lord's questions. I believe Father Matthew Kelty, Chaplain at the Roman Catholic Abbey of Gethsemani in Kentucky, has discovered it (though he would say it was revealed to him):

> In today's Gospel passage there is a very remarkable word from Jesus. Standing with them in the Upper Room, He asks, "Have you anything to eat?" They must have been embarrassed, humiliated, that they had not offered Him hospitality. On the shore of the lake in the early morning fog, He called out to them over the water, "Have you any fish?" The food that Jesus asks of us is our faith in Him. The whole mystical body of Christ is nourished by obedient faith in Him. The Church grows and progresses in vigorous health when we offer Him the bread of faith, the fish of our committed life. To withhold such food, such fish, is to impoverish the Church and humankind. "Have you anything to eat?" We do indeed. "Have you any fish?" We have. And He says, "Bring Me some."
> (Gethsemani Homilies, 2001)

Ponderable

"How beautiful upon the mountains are the feet of him who brings good tidings,' says Isaiah (52:7). Not, how beautiful are the herald's lips which proclaim the good tidings, or his eyes as he proclaims them, or even the good tidings themselves, but how beautiful are the feet – the feet without which he could never have made it up into the mountains, without which the good tidings would never have been proclaimed at all.

Who knows in what inspired way the heart, mind, spirit of the herald came to receive the good tidings of peace and salvation in the first place; but as to the question of whether he would actually do something about them – put his money where his mouth was, his shoe leather where his inspiration was – his feet were the ones that finally had to decide. Maybe it is always so.

When the disciples first came upon the risen Christ that Sunday morning of their confusion and terror, it wasn't His healing hands they touched or His teaching lips or His holy heart. Instead it was those same ruined, tired feet that had carried Him to them three years earlier when they were at their accounts and their nets, that had dragged Him all the way from Galilee to Jerusalem, that had stumbled up the hill where what was to happen happened. 'They took hold of his feet and worshipped him,' Matthew says (28:9). Generally speaking, if you want to know who you really are, as distinct from who you like to think you are, keep an eye on where your feet take you."

(Wishful Thinking: A Theological ABC, Frederick Buechner, 1973)

RESPONSIBLE

Jesus said, "The Son of Man (Jesus' title for Himself) is to come with His angels in the glory of His Father, and then He will repay every person for what they have done." (Matthew 16:27)

We must all appear before the judgment seat of Christ, so that each one may receive good or evil (what each deserves), according to what they have done in the body (during life). (II Corinthians 5:10)

Prayer: *Breathe on me, Breath of God, fill me with life anew, that I may love what Thou dost love, and do what Thou wouldst do. Breathe on me, Breath of God, until my heart is pure, until with Thee I will one will, to do and to endure. Breathe on me, Breath of God, till I am wholly Thine, until this earthly part of me glows with Thy fire divine. Breathe on me, Breath of God, so shall I never die, but live with Thee the perfect life of Thine eternity. (Edwin Hatch, 1886)*

I t was a first for me. Sunday night. T.J. Peppercorns Restaurant at the Hyatt Regency, near the Los Angeles Airport. I arrived late in the afternoon in order to help lead, on Monday and Tuesday, a seminar offered by our denomination's General Assembly on financial stewardship for Ministers of Presbyterian new church developments.

After finishing my soup, I headed to the salad bar. When I returned, my cloth napkin had been re-folded neatly, sitting poised in its triangular shape as it was when I first was seated. It made no sense to me: an exercise in futility. Would the waitress repeat the effort every time I left my chair? Another excursion to the salad bar, watching her this time. I admired how expertly and rapidly she folded.

"Miss," I said as we met in the aisle, "why do you re-fold my napkin?" My puzzlement puzzled her, but she responded, "I'm responsible for making dining here as enjoyable as possible. It's just one of those little things I do to show I'm paying attention to our customers."

I left a big tip.

Andrea Thompson, "Table For Two," (The New Yorker, April 10, 2006) wrote,

> This new restaurant, Country, in the City's Carlton Hotel (90 Madison Avenue at 29th Street) manages to provide consistently enjoyable experiences…the solicitous service extends even beyond the last course. When a guest expressed delight at the apple crumb cake that diners are given on the way out, the host asked, "Would you like another?"

Camelback Inn, Scottsdale, AZ. Earl Grollman, a highly respected Rabbi from Boston, and I are at lunch. Both of us were speakers at the annual convention of the Arizona State Funeral Directors…he on his classic book, Telling a Child About Death, and I on "The Future of the Funeral" (I remain grateful to Dave, of Burton Funeral Homes in Erie, Pennsylvania, who persuaded the National Selected Morticians group to publish a sermon of mine on funeral services, "Joy in the Morning," that led to a series of presentations across the country).

Dr. Grollman was not pleased with his turkey and cheese sandwich…too much fat in the meat, an over-abundance of mayonnaise, wilted lettuce and a tasteless tomato. The waiter made the mistake of responding, "I'm sorry sir, but I just work here."

The Rabbi endeared himself to me by responding gently but firmly,

> Young man, I offer you, unsolicited and without cost, a mini-lesson in life. If the
> sandwiches in this restaurant are going to be consistently good, someone has to
> behave responsibly…like they own the place. And that someone might as well be you.

I'm not sure the crew-cut fellow with the gold-chain necklace understood. You do…don't you?

Quality control, a specialty of Jesus' people: folding napkins… Would you like another?…I don't just work here, I'm responsible for what I serve.

Ponderable

Faithfulness in small things equips us for faithfulness in larger things.

MARTHA
Luke 10:38-42

Prayer: *Now thank we all our God with hearts and hands and voices; Who wondrous things hath done, in Whom His world rejoices; Who, from our mother's arms, hath blessed us on our way with countless gifts of life, and still is ours today. Amen (Martin Rinkart, 1636)*

The jacket of his first book, Bed and Board (1965), describes The Very Reverend Robert Farrar Capon as father of six; Vicar of Christ Church (Episcopal), Port Jefferson, NY; Seminary Professor of Dogmatic Theology and Greek; devoted amateur chamber musician; and wine and food connoisseur. When he published The Foolishness of Preaching – Proclaiming the Gospel Against the Wisdom of the World (1998), I don't know what Father Capon had added to his résumé because all I have from the book are the following two paragraphs contained in a piece of a sermon that drifted across my desk years ago. (I failed to even note the preacher's name who quoted him. Sorry.)

Nevertheless, see what you think....

The incident that immediately precedes Luke 11:1-13 (the Lord's Prayer, the misnamed parable, and the wrap-up in which Jesus says that no matter what you ask for, you're going to get the Holy Spirit) is Jesus' visit to Martha and Mary at the very end of Luke 10. Some quick notes on that visit. First: Martha is a doer. She's as busy as a parish priest: a talker, a cook, a serving girl and a scullery maid, all rolled into one. She's also an Olympic-class petitioner. She's so good at it that she doesn't even ask Jesus for what she wants; she whines to Him, spouting instructions: "Don't you care that my sister's left me to do all the work alone? Tell her to help me!" (10:40) Second: Mary is a listener. She just sits in a swoon at the feet of Jesus and takes Him all in. Third: Jesus reads Martha the riot act for her busyness and praises Mary for doing nothing: "Mary has chosen the good part, which will not be taken away from her." Fourth and last: the whole passage segues perfectly into the Lord's Prayer sequence. The disciples come to Jesus while He's resting, and they ask Him to do something for them (teach them to be spiritual whizzes). Jesus, however, fobs them off with a short Daddy-prayer and then gets down to brass tacks. Real prayer is not asking, He tells them; it's waiting for God to get up from His nap in death and come to you in yours.

Here's something of what I think:

Martha was distracted by much serving: Nancy and Gil Diehl and Janet and Al Kolish modeled early on for me a key to a successful dinner party – make it all appear effortless by preparing ahead as much as possible. A frayed hostess, running helter-skelter around kitchen and dining room, like Martha, encourages guests to feel nearly guilty for causing the host so much work.

Mary sat at the Lord's feet and listened to His teaching: from my seat by the pulpit last Easter morning I was touched by the twenty-six young faces (grades 2-5) in our Children's Choir, only a few feet away. Every eye was riveted, in anticipation, devotion and excitement, on the face and hands of Araminta Montague, their beloved Choir Director, as she led them through a beautiful version of "On Eagle's Wings." During the third Service, I found myself thinking, "I bet Mary's eyes were glued on Jesus' face like these children's are on Araminta's." Are you with me in wondering what the menu was that Martha fretted over? What do you suppose the Lord's teaching to Mary centered on as she sat at His feet? Might it have been something to do with life's priorities, first things first, like Mike Yaconelli reports after a week's Retreat at Toronto's L'Arche Community?

John Blos, one of the members of the handicapped Community, came up to me after one of our first meetings and asked, "Busy?" I said "Yes." He stuck his face right in front of mine and asked, "Why?" He had asked the question I couldn't answer. I didn't know why. Then came the discovery of my soul. Within a few days, I became aware that my whole life was consumed with doing rather than being. I knew what it meant to believe in Jesus. I did not know what it meant to be with Jesus. I knew how to talk about Jesus. I did not know how to sit still long enough to let Jesus talk to me. I found it easy to do the work of God, but I had no idea how to let God work in me. I understood soul-saving, but I was clueless about soul-making. I knew how to be busy, but I did not know how to be still. I could talk about God. I just couldn't listen to God. I felt comfortable with God's people, but I felt uncomfortable alone with God. I was acquainted with the God "out-there," but I was a complete stranger to the God "in-here." I could meet God anywhere… except in my heart, in my soul, in my being. It only took a few hours of silence before I began to hear my soul speaking. It only took being alone for a short period of time for me to discover that I wasn't alone. God had been trying to shout over the noisiness of my life, and I couldn't hear Him. But in the stillness and solitude, His whispers shouted from my soul, "Michael, I am here. I have been calling you. I have been loving you, but you haven't been listening. Can you hear me, Michael? I love you. I have always loved you. And I have been waiting for you to hear Me say that to you. But you have been so busy trying to prove to yourself that you are loved that you have not heard Me." (The Wittenburg Door magazine)

Ponderable

A Short Guide to Lectio Divina
("prayerful reading")

Lectio: Read the passage carefully, getting the sequence and detail without thinking too much about the meaning. Imagine the time of day, season of the year, smells of the land, sounds of the countryside, the human touches – all the elements that would make this scene real to you. Transport yourself into the setting using your imagination.

Meditario: Read the scripture again. Why is there a record of this particular event or saying? What is the significance of this passage in the larger scheme of things? What does this piece mean? How does that affect an understanding of God? Of conduct? Do you see yourself in any of the characters in the passage?

Oratio: Allow your feelings to surface as you read the passage again. Do you feel happy, sad, angry or guilty? Silently or verbally talk this through with God; tell God what you feel about what you have read. Comment in your prayer on anything in the passage to which you respond.

Contemplatio: Sit quietly, breathe deeply and regularly, and let your mind go blank. As you quiet your inner self, simply listen in your heart. If you receive some impression or thought, quietly notice it; then focus your attention on remaining open. If you have no thoughts or impressions, return your mind to the scripture passage. After a while, open your eyes, rested and refreshed, expressing gratitude for your experience.

(Discover Your Spiritual Type: A Guide to Individual and Congregational Growth by Corinne Ware, The Alban Institute, Inc., 1995)

Entrée

Crawfish Pie

½ stick butter
1 cup chopped onions
1/2 cup chopped bell pepper
1/2 cup chopped celery
1-1/2 teaspoons salt
1/2 teaspoon cayenne
1/4 teaspoon black pepper
1/2 cup chopped, seeded, and peeled tomatoes
1 pound crawfish tails
2 tablespoons chopped parsley
2 tablespoons flour
1 cup water
pie crust

Preheat oven to 400°. Melt butter in skillet over medium-high heat. Add onions, bell pepper, celery, salt, cayenne, and black pepper. Sauté for 8 minutes. Add the tomatoes and cook for about 6 minutes, stirring occasionally. Add the crawfish and parsley. Cook, stirring, for about 4 minutes. Dissolve the flour in the water and add to the pan. Stir for about 2 minutes or until mixture thickens. Let cook for at least 30 minutes. Remove from heat. Pour the crawfish mixture into the pie crust and place on a baking sheet. Bake for about 45 minutes. Cool for several minutes.

Yield: 6-8 servings

(Jack Candy)

Soup

Vichyssoise

2 cans cream of potato soup
1 small container of half & half
1 can chicken broth
dash of nutmeg

Combine all ingredients and top with chives. Serve chilled.

Yields: 6

(Beth Williams)

Sauce

Lentil

1-3/4 cups dried brown lentils
2 quarts water
1 cup diced carrots
1-3/4 t. sea salt
dash of dried thyme
2 garlic cloves
2 parsley sprigs
2 bay leaves
2 T. butter
3 cups chopped onion
1 t. cumin
6 cups or more spinach
1 T. fresh lemon juice
1/2 t. black pepper

Sort and wash lentils. Combine lentils, water, and next 6 ingredients in a large pot. Bring to a boil, cover, and reduce heat. Simmer 45 minutes or until tender. Melt butter in a large skillet. Add the onion and cumin; sauté 10 minutes or until browned. Stir onion into lentil mixture. Discard bay leaves. Add spinach; simmer uncovered until spinach is tender. Remove soup from heat and stir in juice and pepper.

Yields: 6 servings

(David Glover)

EXPERIMENT
John 1:35-46

Table Grace: *Around this table, Lord, as we enjoy our food which comes from Thee, may love with all things good be found, and grateful thanks to Thee abound. Amen. (Stuart R. Oglesby, Prayers for All Occasions, 1940)*

The cover story by Jerry Shriver in the "Life" section of USA Today (December 8, 2005), carries the catchy title, "Incredible and Edible – Adventurous Chefs Push the Envelope, Then Eat It." The lengthy article contains lines like these:

> These chefs are committed to reinvigorating the art of eating….They seem to
> share a boredom with traditional cooking, questioning and reinterpreting every
> aspect of food preparation and dining….Have technique, understand the basics,
> use common sense, use your eyes and tongue, but be free….There is an enormous
> distinction between innovation and something that is deliberately eccentric.

Were you thinking of the institutional Church ("a boredom with the traditional") or of your relationship with Jesus ("questioning and reinterpreting") as you read the above? I did, and do.

I speak frequently of my vision, which I trust is Christ's, for McDonough Presbyterian Church being rooted but not buried in the past…of "Old Traditions, New Beginnings"… of ways to reinvigorate our spiritual lives. Seldom, however, do I have concrete ideas, methods, programs, approaches in mind. It is, I suspect, the willingness to experiment that is a vital key to Christian growth, personally and in the life of a congregation. As a chef says in the USA Today article, "Understand the basics, use common sense…but be free!" Or, as Oz Clarke, wine expert, writes,

> Don't be afraid to experiment. Who would guess that salty Roquefort
> cheese and rich, sweet sauternes would go together. But they do, and
> it's a match made in heaven. (Pocket Wine Guide, 2005)

Much more significantly, it is the Lord's invitation/command, issued to the disciples of John the Baptizer, then echoed by Philip and Nathaniel, "Come and see." The willingness to experiment with the promises and claims of God's Son, to be free and open to the possibility that something good can come out of Nazareth, assists God's Spirit to empower us to take yet another step in discipleship.

Our eldest daughter, Deborah, now in her early forties, refuses to try turkey. Daughter Sheri, late thirties, has yet to experiment with the taste of liver. Youngest of the clan in her mid-twenties, Heather will not permit a mushroom to cross her lips. The child in your highchair has her/his own list of rejected food items…rejected without even sampling them. Some Wednesday nights at the church when we gather weekly for dinner, I watch, intrigued as youngsters, with their parents, make their way through the meal line to fill their plates with goodies that our Kitchen Coordinator, Sherry, and her staff have prepared. Small heads regularly shake No! to many of the food offerings. Just try a bite, I want to say to the child or teenager. You'll never know unless you risk it a bit…experiment.

Ponderable

THE GREAT SPIRITUAL
EXPERIMENT
Three Weeks Experimenting
With The Claims And Promises Of Jesus

Dear Friends In The Faith Journey,

This "Experiment" is based on the conviction that the Bible is God's unique and authoritative written Word to us. Therefore, we can trust what the Scriptures say. For these three weeks, please work on the assumption that the assigned verses for each day are true. Put into daily practice the claims and promises about which you read. At the conclusion of the "Experiment" make your final decision as to whether or not Jesus is who He says He is, and can do what He says He can do. I am certain that this "putting Christ to the test" will convince, or reconvince, you that God's Son deserves our loyalty!

(All Chapters And Verses Are From Mark's Gospel)

First Week

Day 1 1:1, 7-11 *(Jesus is announced as God's Son)*
Day 2 1:14-20 *(Jesus' invitation: "Follow Me!")*
Day 3 2:5-12 *(Claim Jesus' promise to forgive sin)*
Day 4 3:24-25 *(What "division in your house" needs repair?)*
Day 5 3:35 *(How to be Christ's "brother/sister!")*
Day 6 4:1-20 *(What is your "soil type"?)*
Day 7 4:30-32 *(How can you assist the "seed's" growth in you?)*

Second Week

Day 1 5:19 *(Tell someone today what the Lord has done for you)*
Day 2 5:34 *(What needs to be "healed" in you today?)*
Day 3 6:1-6 *(Is unbelief hindering God's work in your life?)*
Day 4 6:30-32 *(Make a spiritually "quiet time" for yourself today)*
Day 5 7:20-23 *(Accept the call to change an inner attitude)*
Day 6 8:27-29 *(Life's most important question!)*
Day 7 8:34-38 *(A call to reorganize our priorities)*

Third Week

Day 1 9:23-24 *(Belief in Jesus does not remove all doubt!)*
Day 2 9:35;10:43-45 *(How to be first in Jesus' Kingdom)*
Day 3 10:27 *(Be encouraged!)*
Day 4 11:22-25 *(A promise concerning prayer)*
Day 5 12:28-34 *(Love God more than anyone or anything else)*
Day 6 14:36 *(Doing God's will is life's most important decision)*
Day 7 16:1-7 *(The resurrected Jesus is alive in our world, waiting for us to join Him by serving others!)*

SABBATH

…in six days the Lord made heaven and earth, and on the seventh day God rested, and was refreshed. (Exodus 31:17b)

Prayer: *Great God, we bow in Your presence. May Your Word be our rule, Your Spirit our Teacher and Your greater glory our supreme concern. Amen!*

And on the seventh day God finished creating, and God rested on the seventh day from all the work which God had done. God blessed the seventh day, and hallowed it… (Genesis 2:2-3)

Why did God rest on the seventh day? Was He tired? God, the mighty God, the all-powerful Creator…exhausted? We'll return to that intriguing possibility in just a moment.

But first, another interesting question, at least to me: what did God do on the seventh day, the day God hallowed, the day of rest? If God had listened to my grandfather, a minister in the old northern United Presbyterian Church, there would have been very little God was allowed to do on – as they always called it – the Sabbath day. No ball games or movies…no radio (TV was still a fantasy), no card or board games, no work of any kind, including the cooking of food – that all had to be done on Saturday, certainly no shopping. To me, a Presbyterian youth in the early-to-mid-1950's it seemed like all you were permitted to do on the Sabbath – the seventh day – was go to church.

To a Presbyterian of any age in the twenty-first century, that idea of "Sabbath observance," as it still was called in my youth growing up in the home of a Presbyterian minister, is out-dated, impractical. Or, is it? Maybe there is more to this idea of a seventh day of rest than meets some of our eyes.

Who couldn't do with a restful day? And what if God intended the Sabbath observance to be a blessing, not a burden? Don't most, if not all, of us live under the tyranny of time? Isn't Steve McCutchan, Minister of Highland Presbyterian Church in Winston-Salem, North Carolina, on target when he describes "time's tyrannical control of our lives" using these words,

> There are few realities more oppressive and dehumanizing than the crush of time. The last fifteen years have witnessed the increasing pressurization of our lives. Even our advances in technology, instead of freeing us, have served to increase the pressure. We have meetings over breakfast, lunch and dinner. Fast food restaurants and microwaves reduce waiting. We have installed telephones in our cars so we can do business while driving. Computers force us to deal with far more information than we can comprehend

and fax machines mean that we don't have to wait for the mail. Businesses are open
seven days a week and often at least sixteen hours a day. The effect of all that pressure
in our society is easy to see.

If we agree with that assessment of the tyranny of time, we're ready to take up the question with which I opened, "Why did God rest on the seventh day from all the work of creation He had done?" Was God tired?! Yes, I believe God was exhausted! God rested on the Sabbath Day, the seventh day, because God was worn out from all the work.

I think that was the case because of this unusual word, translated "refreshed", in our text from Exodus 31:17,
…on the seventh day God rested and was refreshed.

That Hebrew word, "nephesh", usually translated refreshed, is a verb form which means soul or life. The extremely able Presbyterian scholar and author in the area of Old Testament studies, Walter Brueggeman, recently retired from our denomination's Columbia Theological Seminary here in Atlanta, says the last words of Exodus 31:17 literally mean that God rested in order to get God's "soul" back! The Biblical point seems clear: God's work of creation was so tiring that even the mighty, all-powerful Creator needed rest and "refreshment"…needed an opportunity to get spirit and soul back to full strength!

You are not at all surprised now to hear me suggest that if God needed the seventh day, our Sunday…our Lord's Day…as a holy day of rest, it's more than likely we do, too.

God gave Him/Herself the seventh day as a blessing…a holy day of rest from work. God gives us the Sabbath even today not as a burden, in terms of what is and what is not permitted, but as a blessing. Sunday – the Lord's Day – the Sabbath – the seventh day – a day of rest/refreshment from our work, and a day of special communion with God the refreshed Creator…a blessing!

You certainly do not need me to spell out details of what it means for us to observe the Sabbath today. You are more than able to make those decisions. I offer, however, a guideline for your deciding: Think of the first day of the week as a change-of-pace day.

Sunday, rest and refreshment: Get up and gather with God's people in worship and church school…a change-of-pace from the usual work routine of the other six days. Then do what you want to do, not what you have to do: that's a change of pace from the other six days, too.

Doing what we want, rather than must do, is what true leisure is all about. Leisure, from the Latin "licere", meaning at its root, "to be permitted". Real leisure, therefore, is giving ourselves permission to use time as we want to, instead of what is required of us.

Keeping the Sabbath Day holy is one of God's gracious blessings. By observing the seventh day as "leisure" time to honor God by resting from our work, we fight the tyranny of time over all our days… and we experience something of what our text tells us is God's truth,

…on the seventh day God rested, and was refreshed….
(God got spirit and soul back to full strength!)

As always, God set the best example.

Ponderable

Ways to Remember the Sabbath
(From Sabbath, by Wayne Miller)

Bless your children.
Place your hands gently on their heads and offer your blessing. Let them hear your prayers for their happiness.

Seek companionship.
One of the most precious gifts we can offer is to be a place of refuge, a Sabbath for one another.

Reset your inner compass.
Make a list of values and principles that guide your life.

Dessert 🍧

Amaretto Ice Cream Sandwich

In a 3-quart Pyrex dish:
2 T. Amaretto – drizzle in bottom of dish
1 pkg. ice cream sandwiches – place over Amaretto

I buy the Mayfield mini sandwiches,
16 count per package, and usually have 2 left over.

1/4 cup Amaretto – drizzle over sandwiches

In a mixing bowl:
2 cups whipping cream
1/2-3/4 tsp. almond extract
1 3.3 oz. pkg. white chocolate pudding – add slowly

Mix those three items together with a mixer or wand, then add:
1/4 cup Amaretto – stir in
12 oz. Cool Whip – defrosted; stir in
1 6oz. bag of Heath Bits (has chocolate on these)
1 71/2 oz. bag of "Bits o Brittle" (no chocolate)

These are hard to find. If you cannot
find them, use two bags of Heath Bits.

Spread mixture over sandwiches. Freeze 2 hours, then cover and freeze 6 hours more. Must freeze 8 hours, but can be frozen up to 2 weeks. Usually best before 3 days.

When serving, cut and drizzle Magic Shell chocolate coating on top. (Cut a small hole in top of paper to drizzle, otherwise it would be too much.)

(Sherri Gamble)

Vegetable 🍽

Herb-Roasted Potatoes

12 new red potatoes (about 2 pounds) cut into wedges
1/4 cup olive oil
2 garlic cloves, pressed
1 t. salt
1 t. ground cumin
1/2 t. paprika
1/4 t. dried oregano
1/8 t. ground red pepper

Toss together all ingredients in a large bowl; spread mixture evenly into a lightly greased, aluminum foil-lined 13 x 9-inch baking dish. Bake at 425°F for 30 minutes.

Yield: 6 to 8 servings

(Helen Albright)

Entrée 🍖

Horseradish Crusted Pork Chops

1½-inch-thick pork chops
2 cloves garlic, minced
1 t. chopped rosemary
1 t. chopped thyme
2 T. olive oil
1 t. salt
½ t. pepper
1 t. olive oil

In large sealed bag, mix together garlic, herbs and 2 T. olive oil. Add chops and seal; refrigerate overnight. Remove chops from bag and season with salt and pepper. Heat oven to 450°F. Heat the 1 t. oil in skillet over medium-high heat. Add chops and cook for 5 minutes on each side. Remove chops to baking dish; top each chop with horseradish crust and place in oven for 6-9 minutes until brown.

Horseradish crust: In bowl, beat together 1 stick softened butter, 6 T. horseradish, ¼ t. pepper and 1 cup breadcrumbs.

(Lisa Glover)

78

DINERS
Luke 19

Table Grace: Our Father, bless us as we eat, let love make every morsel sweet. We thank Thee for Thy gifts this day. May all our needs be met, we pray. Amen. (Prayers for All Occasions, Stuart T. Oglesby, 1940)

It's one of two restaurants in town, the only one open on Sundays. Cafeteria style. Today's offerings: turkey, fried chicken or hamburger "steak" smothered in gravy; stuffing; black-eyed peas; collards, fried okra, and green beans; cranberry sauce; macaroni and cheese; cornbread and mashed potatoes; lemon meringue and sweet potato pies; tea and water. Luncheon special ($5.19): one meat, two vegetables, bread. It's Mom's Kitchen, in Plains, Georgia; just a block from Billy's (as in Carter) Gas Station which is currently being renovated as a historical site. "Mom's" reminded me of an old-fashioned diner.

A yellowed page torn from a magazine article (it may have been The Smithsonian – I regret not keeping the entire piece with the author's name), makes these observations about diners:

> The diner represents democracy. It's everyone's kitchen. It speaks of good
> and ample – if not fancy – food and friendly prices. Diners are unpretentious
> and tolerant places where no one holds it against you if you don't wear a tie,
> or if you do. No reservations, wine lists, candles, maitre d' in a tux, or "Please
> Wait To Be Seated" signs, and the waitress calls you "Hon"….There are no
> pretensions in a diner. The garbage man sits next to the college president
> and the chief of police sits next to the long-haired kid.

In March 5, 2006, it was Dave (retired farmer from Iowa, 81 years young), Mark (high school student), Arlen (Quaker Pastor) and I sitting at Mom's Diner/Kitchen almost next to Jimmy and Rosalyn Carter. The 39th President was dressed unpretentiously, as he had been while teaching the 10 a.m. Sunday School class (on Psalm 8…a wonderfully helpful presentation) and during the 11 a.m. worship Service at Maranatha Baptist Church: navy suit, powder blue shirt open at the neck, and bolo ("cowboy tie"). His bride of nearly 60 years in black slacks, blouse and brown/black jacket.

The Carter's table guests were two missionaries from Honduras and a couple from Nicaragua, as well as a former Georgia Senator (long-time friend of the Carters) and his family. All had also spent the morning at Sunday School and worship. Of course, four Secret Service personnel conspicuously dressed, guarded the President's table, while military men – bomb squad specialists and their dog – patrolled the diner's grounds.

In Jesus' earthly days you were judged, in large part, by those with whom you ate. I believe Jesus' judgment of us today includes a similar criterion.

When the Lord startled Zacchaeus, the despised Jewish turncoat tax collector who had sold out to the hated occupation forces of Rome, by inviting Himself to lunch,
The crowd saw it and they all murmured, "Jesus has gone to be the guest of a man who is a sinner."
(Luke 19:7)

I suspect they more than "murmured." It seems most never got the message that the Messiah excludes no one, especially from table fellowship. God's Son owns and operates a diner. We call it the Church of Jesus Christ. Welcome. Sit with Rosalyn and Jimmy, natives of Nicaragua and Honduras, Senator and Secret Service, the Quaker and Presbyterian, youthful and aged, and all manner of the Day of Pentecost guests (Acts 2 – Parthian and Medes and E'lamites and residents of Mesopotamia and….) It's called "Church."

Youngest daughter Heather and husband Dee have developed a Christmas Eve tradition of hosting a few folks for dinner between our 5 p.m. and 11:15 p.m. worship services at McDonough Presbyterian Church. The guest list varies annually, but always included are one or two without family or significant friends available…who, if not invited, might remain lonely in their sycamore tree. Heather's meals are creative and delicious, but the best taste is that the dinner table feels like a diner – like Jesus intends His church to be.

Ponderable

The common meal is a primary, maybe the primary way by which we take care of our physical need for food, our social need for conversation and intimacy, and our cultural need to carry on traditions and convey values – what philosopher Albert Borgmann calls "the culture of the table." The meal – preparation, serving, eating, cleaning up – has always been a microcosm of the Gospel. (Eugene H. Peterson, Journal for Preachers, Easter, 2002)

PREACHER

Jesus said, "…preach as you go, saying, 'The Kingdom of God is at hand.' " (Matthew 10:7)
Preach the Word, be urgent in season and out of season; convince, rebuke, exhort….(II Timothy 4:2)

Prayer: *Behold, Lord, an empty vessel that needs to be filled. My Lord, fill it. I am weak in the faith; strengthen me. I am cold in love; warm me and make me fervent, that my love may go out to my neighbor. I do not have a strong and firm faith; at times I doubt and am unable to trust You altogether. O Lord, help me. Strengthen my faith and trust in You. In You I have sealed the treasure of all I have. I am poor; You are rich and came to be merciful to the poor. I am a sinner; You are upright. With me, there is an abundance of sin; in You is the fullness of righteousness. Therefore I will remain with You, of Whom I can receive, but to whom I may not give. Amen. (Martin Luther, 16th century Protestant Reformer)*

Father, grandfather, three uncles, and a cousin, all Presbyterian Ministers…a family business, in the best sense. It has been suggested that I must have felt pressured by that tradition to go into the ministry yourself. No, not at all. In fact, it was a Muskingum College history professor, David Sturdivant (who insisted he was agnostic) who, my in junior year as a history major, put the possibility to me most directly: "I think you would make a good clergyman; the Church certainly needs them! Have you considered applying to Seminary?"

"It must have been rough growing up as a P.K." other's hinted. It didn't feel that way to me, although my sister, Kathy, disagreed. I thought there were advantages…similar to the ones I've felt all my ordained years: People had/have expectations of me as the "preacher's kid" and as a clergyman, and that has helped me live a better life than I might have otherwise.

I've been fascinated lately by as beautiful a book as I have ever received (Lisa and David Glover's gift), Van Gogh's Table at the Auberge Ravoux, Recipes From the Artist's Last Home and Paintings of Café Life (Alexandra Leaf and Fred Leeman, 2001). The writing style, photographs, reproductions of his artwork, and information are superb! Vincent Van Gogh also was a preacher's kid and clergyman who felt differently about the calling than I do:

Van Gogh realized that an artistic career would not only deprive him of family life, but
also put him on the fringe of polite society. He was far from scared to leave the protection
of his family, the preachers, art dealers and admirals he had grown up among. As a
preacher in the Borinage, 1879, he had been used to subjecting himself to, even
indulging himself in, physical hardship and mingling with his social inferiors.

I've not been deprived of family life; have avoided physical hardships; and never thought of others as being my social inferiors. I haven't a clue as to what Van Gogh's training was, or what the year of ministry was about, but it doesn't sound like a good experience. I do know that he, in his lifetime, sold only one of his 800 or so paintings, and his first one-man show wasn't until after he was dead (at age 37, by suicide). Take heart, all ye who feel unrecognized and unappreciated in this life!

I do know, as well, that unlike me, Van Gogh was not a foodie. Said the innkeeper of the café where he lodged for a period, "He regularly took meals with us. We served simple food: meat, vegetables, salad, dessert. He had no culinary preferences. He never sent a dish back."

The authors continue at another place:

> Van Gogh's relationship with food was complicated. Like his fellow Protestants
> he equated virtue with abstinence from luxury. This held especially true for
> food, which he often reduced to its essence, bread.

Many of us who delight in preparing, serving, and enjoying fine food are discovering that frequently the simplest, most basic, uncomplicated recipes are a hit.

If preacher means, as I believe, one who proclaims, by word and deed, the redemptive life of Jesus of Nazareth, God's Son, then all Christians are called to preach. It's just that we have different pulpits. But the sermon is, or should be, the same. I think Frederick Buechner, Presbyterian Minister, whose pulpit is the writer's desk, sums up best what preachers of every flavor must announce, uncomfortable as it is to many:

> If the world is sane, then Jesus is mad as a hatter and the Last Super is the Mad Tea
> Party. The world says, "Mind your own business," and Jesus says, "There is no such
> thing as your own business." The world says, "Follow the wisest course and be a success,"
> and Jesus says, "Follow Me and be crucified." The world says, "Drive carefully – the life
> you save may be your own," and Jesus says, "Whoever would save his life will lose it,
> and whoever loses his life for My sake will find it." The world says, "Law and order,"
> and Jesus says, "Love." The world says, "Get," and Jesus says, "Give." In terms of the
> world's sanity, Jesus is crazy as a coot, and anybody who thinks he can follow Him
> without being a little crazy too is laboring less under the cross than under a delusion.
> "We are fools for Christ's sake," Paul says, faith says – the faith that ultimately the
> foolishness of God is wiser than the wisdom of men, the lunacy of Jesus saner
> than the grim sanity of the world. (The Faces of Jesus)

 Ponderable   "When I was in my late teens, I wanted to be a preacher. When I was in my late twenties, I wanted to be a good preacher. Now that I am older, I want more than anything else to be a Christian. To live simply, to love generously, to speak truthfully, to serve faithfully and leave everything else to God." (Fred B. Craddock)

PIZZA
I Kings 17:8-12a / Mark 6:30-34

Prayer:

Thank You, God, for all these things that reveal Your love. Thank You for the heavens that cover us, for the earth beneath our feet, for the sun in the day and the stars of the night, for the snow and the rains and the rivers and the lakes, for mountains and valleys and trees and flowers. Thank You, God, for those people who demonstrate Your love. Thank You for those great men and women who followed You throughout history, for the priests and prophets and apostles and ministers, for doctors and teachers and mothers and fathers and painters and musicians and writers and farmers and laborers and clerks, for those men and women who accepted Your love and dedicated their lives to living for others. Thank You, God, for choosing me to be one of Your people, for calling me and equipping me to communicate Your love to my world. Thank You, God. Amen. (Psalm 136, Translated by Leslie F. Brandt)

In the opening section each week of The New Yorker, all in too-tiny print for my decaying eyes, is a quarter page titled, "Table for Two," reviewing one of the City's restaurants or other food providers. A pizza guy, John (Kid) Lynch, works the streets of New York City selling, from his kitchen on wheels, freshly made pizza. As good as his is, Kid insists, "L & B Spumoni in Bensonhurst is where God goes for pizza."

I think it's more likely God calls the Sons of Italy Hall in Ellwood City, Pennsylvania for take-out, requesting their white pizza. Forget the tomato sauce. Pizza crust is best, as far as I'm concerned, with extra virgin olive oil, freshly sautéed garlic, kosher salt and ground white pepper. If your taste buds match mine, ask to have a few anchovies and/or kalamata olives, as toppings. Enjoy!

I've decided – I have no scholarly support for my position – that the bread/cake and oil mentioned in I Kings 17 was an early version of pizza crust and fine olive oil. I agree: That's a silly guess, but let's go with it anyway. The story, like a number of other Biblical accounts, is a bit weird: Hide yourself, Elijah, by the brook called Cherith (says God)....The ravens will feed you there (I thought people fed birds, not vice-versa)....Now move on to Zarephath; a widow there will feed you.

God's prophet (spokesman) requests of the widow water and bread. She tells him that her pantry is nearly bare and she has plans to use the last of her oil and meal (white pizza) for herself and her dying son. Read on for yourself and discover the happy ending.

Let the lesson from the table, white pizza or not, be God's call to extravagance (with appreciation to Matthew Kelty, Gethsemani Homilies). Noting Mark 6, the account of the widow's mite, Father Kelty writes,

> Perhaps Jesus' disciples made disparaging remarks about the widow and her gift. Christ frequently took up passing comments, showing that even by their own standards the disciples did not make sense. "Why choose the best seat? You may be asked to move lower." No one became honorable by looking important, being prominent. That is no route to honor. It's the way of the world though. Big people drive big cars. We Christians are called to be big. Not in the way of the world, but in the way of the widow and her mite – extravagant – in the way of the widow gathering sticks, bringing water to Elijah and bread, though she uses the last of what little she has for him. Extravagant woman. Like the poor Jesus Who stripped Himself of glory to become poor for our sake that He might lead us to glory and eternal riches in Him. Extravagant! So the call is to extravagance, not prudence; not shrewd calculation. We can do it once in a while. Doing it once in a while makes it possible to do it once and for all when we make a leap of faith and accept Jesus wholly. It is an extravagance we never regret and never renege on. This and this alone makes life worth living. The two widows were on to something. One hopes we are. And if we are, there is no hiding it. If you're stingy, you never get the message. No one who has drunk the wine of extravagance will ever stoop to stinginess on anything.

Ponderable

"If giving causes more pain than pleasure, it is not our money but our faith that is insufficient."
(William Sloan Coffin, Credo)

DEADLY
Galatians 5:13-25

Prayer: *Almighty God, You know all needs before we speak our prayers, yet You welcome our concerns for others in Jesus Christ. Especially we pray for those who keep watch over the sick and dying…those who weep with the grieving…those who are without faith and cannot accept Your love…those who grow old. As You have made this day, O God, You also make the night. Give light for our comfort. Come upon us with quietness and still our souls that we may listen for the whisper of Your Spirit and be attentive to Your nearness in our dreams. Amen. (Daily Prayer – Supplemental Liturgical Resource 5, Presbyterian Church, USA)*

The list of the Seven Deadly Sins was concocted by the Italian poet, Dante Alighieri (1265-1321), in his masterpiece, Divine Comedy, completed in his final years. You may know it is an imaginary trip through hell and paradise. Dante's reading of the New Testament lead him to conclude that the following sins were the most "deadly,"

• Pride   • Envy   • Anger   • Greed   • Sloth   • Gluttony   • Lust

How has it come to be, for some of our sisters and brothers in the faith, that a ranking of "deadly sins," or "the works of the flesh" (Galatians 5), is acceptable? Where is it written that the obese Elder's sin of gluttony is more acceptable to God than the Deacon's lust that results in a sinful affair? Who determined to lift up the sin of homosexuality of the seminarian seeking ordination as a Minister, but downplay the sin of idolatry exhibited by the Christian business person who worships first at the altar of financial success?

I'm in that old-fashioned school of theology that believes the Bible teaches there is Sin, and then there are sins: All sins (unranked) result from Sin. I know what my prejudices are – what sins I find more detestable than others – but I can't find sufficient Biblical material to justify my priorities. Sin is deadly, regardless of the sins.

Sin will take us further than we want to go, keep us longer than we
want to stay, and cost us more than we want to pay. (Author unknown)

Consider breakfast at Don and Lloyd's condo (Make this transition with me, please): continental breakfast (freshly-squeezed orange juice and just-perked coffee, a croissant with butter) waiting on the counter of the guest bathroom as the two men left for work. It wasn't the food as much as it was the love that prompted it. These were the days when nearly all of us practiced "don't ask, don't tell." Two gay guys, professing Christians, committed to a "till death do us part" relationship, hosting me for two months at the most miserable, painful, and pain-causing time of my life when I was censured for a year from practicing ordained ministry as punishment for the sin of divorcing. My parents temporarily abandoned me…Presbyterian clergy colleagues were not heard from (with the blessed exception of Bill Jackson, and later, Bob Downs and Bob McCrumb)... Presbytery Executive John, "Pastor to the Pastors," (sic) requested I sign a pledge that I would not try to take members from the large-in-number church I was serving and form my own congregation...none of my straight Christian friends contacted me – except Bob Traister, a fringe member of the Church about to end his second marriage – who rescued me by creating a sales job in Columbus, Ohio, with the James Austin Company.

But Lloyd and Don were there, caring for me, encouraging me. Always respecting my privacy. Preparing delightful evening meals. Taking me out to dinner. They knew what it felt like to "be on the outside," ostracized.

If you ask me what I believe about homosexuality, I'm prone to quip, "Exactly what Jesus did," (See if you can find anything in the Gospels about the matter), and then refer you to William Sloan Coffin,

> It is not Scripture that creates hostility to homosexuality, but rather hostility to homosexuals that prompts some Christians to recite a few sentences from Paul and retain passages from an otherwise discarded Old Testament law code. In abolishing slavery and in ordaining women we've gone beyond biblical literalism. It's time we did the same with gays and lesbians. The problem is not how to reconcile homosexuality with scriptural passages that condemn it, but rather how to reconcile the rejection and punishment of homosexuals with the love of Christ. It can't be done. So instead of harping on what's "natural," let's talk of what's "normal," what operates according to the norm. For Christians the norm is Christ's love. If people can show the tenderness and constancy in caring that honors Christ's love, what matters their sexual orientation? Shouldn't a relationship be judged by its inner worth rather than its outer appearance? When has a monopoly on durable life-warming love been held only by legally wed heterosexuals? (Credo)

Ponderable

"Scott Levy, a pastor in the Midwest, was preaching for a pastor friend one Sunday morning. He went early to the church to see what it was like and get the feel of the atmosphere. As he was walking down a long hallway, his sermon notes in one hand and his pulpit robe draped over the other arm, he came upon a large room used as a nursery for preschoolers. Glancing in, he saw a little boy who looked about four years old, sitting all by himself. The little boy said, 'Hi, my name's Tommy, and I'm all alone in this big room.' Scott, who had done a lot of counseling, decided to use his nondirective counseling technique on the little boy. He answered back, 'You feel all alone in this room?' 'I don't just feel it,' said the little boy. 'I know I am all alone!' Trying to reassure the boy, Scott replied confidently, 'Don't you worry now. I'm sure that before too long somebody will come to be with you.' With wistful eyes, little Tommy looked up at him and said, 'Why not you?'" (As told by James W. Moore, Can You Remember to Forget?)

MEMORIES

Remember that the Lord your God brought you out of slavery in Egypt. (Deuteronomy 5:15)
Remember the Sabbath day, to keep it holy. (Exodus 20:8)
Remember the words of the Lord Jesus…Do this to remember Me. (Acts 20:35, I Corinthians 11:24)

Prayer: *(Father): Bless ye. (Answer): Bless ye. (Father): The eyes of all wait upon Thee, O Lord; (Answer): And Thou givest them their meat in due season. (Father): Thou openest Thine hand; (Answer): And fillest all things living with plenteousness. (Father): Glory be to the Father, and to the Son, and to the Holy Ghost; (Answer): As it was in the beginning, is now, and ever shall be, world without end. Amen. (Father): Let us pray. Bless, O Lord, these gifts to our use, and us to Thy service, through Christ our Lord. (Answer): Amen. (A Child): Bid, Sir, a blessing. (Father): May the King of Eternal glory make us partakers of His heavenly table. (Answer): Amen. (Robert Farrar Capon, Bed and Board)*

A tiny radio station, WFEM, in Ellwood City, Pennsylvania, in the 1980's played the golden oldies and broadcast local high school football games. It took some persuasion, but eventually the Session of North Sewickley Presbyterian Church agreed to purchase a half-hour of air time weekly, at $10 a pop, to broadcast cassette tapes of my sermons. It didn't last long because no Elder ever heard anyone comment that they listened to their preacher on the radio. What has lasted for me is the slogan WFEM went by: "The more you listen, the more you remember" ….referring, I guess, to listening to the oldie songs and remembering those days.

It's true, don't you think? The more I listen to my past, reminisce, shuffle through my memories, the more I remember, recall of sad/glad experiences that remain challenging/comforting today.

Have you been intentional lately about remembering? You might be pleased by setting a bit of time aside soon to revisit some memories. As expected, Peter J. Gomes, preacher to Harvard University, says it well,

St. Paul always invites his listeners to acts of remembrance, constantly reminding people to remember "Remember what it was like before you knew Christ. Remember what it was like when you were young in the faith, or frightened, or intimidated, or new." Even more, throughout all of his writings, St. Paul invites people to remember their moments of victory, of achievement, of success, of pleasure, of satisfaction. He invites us to remember those precious moments in our lives. Remember what the Lord has done for you, remember what you have done for the Lord, remember what others have done for you, and remember what you have done for others. Memory is the great key to this enterprise. We are to remember these moments because in them we find evidence of God's presence and activity in our lives. To remember is to be reminded, even in our loneliness, that we have never been alone, abandoned, or forgotten. It is the essence of religion to remember, for it is in recollection that we find out – that is, remember, or put back together – how on a rare occasion or two we have acted nobly, honorably, with purity of thought and heart, performed excellently, responded graciously; and just as it will surprise you to discover how good God has been to you, it will also surprise you to discover those moments in your own lives. (Strength For the Journey, Biblical Wisdom For Daily Living, 2003)

A surprise for me not long ago, as I checked in with my memory bank, was the frequency with which food was central to the remembrance.

Hattie's Hamburger Hut, Torch Lake, Michigan: weekly outing treat during our family's annual August vacation…a good family time in my life…. Heather, in her fifth year, ordering shrimp cocktail at Ohio's Youngstown Club on Grandpa's check – what a gift Dorothy's folks were to us, young parents…. My dad's mother, New Wilmington, Pennsylvania: When we visited, she prepared dates filled with cream cheese, and peanuts and black coffee (adults only) boiled on the stove; It's been a blessing to come from Presbyterian clergy roots (grandfather, dad, three uncles, a cousin)…. Jack, taking me for a week as his guest to the exclusive Duquesne Hunting and Fishing Club, Canada: top-shelf fishing guides, special worms flown in from New England, shore lunches, cooks (I still taste her blueberry – freshly picked – pie); what it meant to be treated royally by my wife's father…. Rummel Creek Elementary School, Houston, Texas: with Dorothy, making special lunches to surprise grandsons Bradon, Miller, and Anderson at the school's cafeteria; lovely words of introduction around the tables: This is my Grandpa Dudley and Grandma Dorothy…. Tom and Mary Sterrett, Jim's relatives, Letterkenny County, Donegal, Ireland: Arrangements were made for a brief morning visit at their small farm; Jim to renew acquaintance, Dorothy and me to meet the older couple for the first time; arrived at the agreed upon hour, 10 a.m; greeted enthusiastically by the Scots who migrated to Ireland; seated in living room; cookies and homemade goodies served with Scotch (remember: 10 a.m.!); It would have been rude not to partake (None of us would have needed an early nap if Mary had quit refilling our tumblers!) traveling with friends can be such a delightful and eye-opening experience…. Jim and Mary Lou Trotter's farm, Enon Valley, Ohio: harnessing the ponies to sulkies and exercising them on the homemade track (I once was the only clergyman in Pennsylvania licensed by the National Pony Trotters Association) while women and children picked and prepared sweet corn, followed by a trip to the Dairy Queen for dessert; a lovely diversion and a taste of life on a dairy farm with generous and enjoyable parishioners who "let me be myself," and not just their pastor…. Bob and Sally McCrumb, Mars, Pennsylvania: insisting that occasionally the Rose Clan gather at their place, Poverty Point Farm (sheep) for a reunion – family ties, even if strained, seem to become more significant as deaths of loved ones increase…. Bob and Carla Traister, Flagler Beach, Florida: with Dorothy and me, and Fritz and Cindy Lacroix, spent many a Thanksgiving Day meal together; This year Carla was recovering from breast cancer, the other couple had to be away and Dorothy was checking on her mom in Ohio (Alzheimer's Unit); I drove three early Thanksgiving morning hours to meet Bob and Carla at a restaurant for lunch – traditions are worth the effort.
The more you listen, the more you remember.

Life is not a journey to the grave with the intention of arriving safely in a pretty and well-preserved body, but rather to skid in broadside, thoroughly used up, totally worn out, and proclaiming, "Wow, what a ride!!!" (Casual Living catalogue) Or, as Fred Buechner says, "Spending your life for Christ like a drunken sailor on leave."

Ponderable

TOQUE

"Search me, O God, and know my heart." (Psalm 139:23)
"…God knows the secrets of the heart…" (Psalm 44:21)

Prayer: *O God, source of all holy fires, bless the story of my day. Enlighten and warm my heart. Amen.*
(A Celtic prayer)

July 22, 2006, I made my typical weekly morning trip (during the season) to Atlanta's only organic Farmer's Market. It's the area's chefs who offers a 9:30-10 a.m. cooking demonstration that draws me. This Saturday was quite special. The newest chef at The Dining Room (Ritz-Carlton, Buckhead), Arnaud Berthelier, a youthful native of Nancy in northwest France, demonstrated how to do wonderful things with a slice of tomato. For the record: I shook his hand afterwards, nearly bowing as I muttered, "Thank you, Chef." For a foodie like me, it was nearly the same as an adoring Roman Catholic kissing the Pope's ring.

Footnote: Only fourteen restaurants in 2006 in the U.S. received a Mobil Five-Star rating. While most cities have never had one winner, Atlanta has had two: The Dining Room and Seeger's (Guenter Seeger is a former Dining Room chef).

In preparation for Chef Berthelier's presentation, I read Christiane Lauterbach's article in Atlanta magazine's article, "Savoir Faire," about the prestigious Ritz Dining Room. These sentences puzzled me:

> Chef Berthelier, who arrived in September, 2005, is the latest star in a spectacular line.
> Like his predecessor, he would not be caught dead wearing a toque.

What in the dickens is a toque? The Internet's (Google) answer is,

> **Toque:** Etymology: Middle French, a soft hat with a narrow brim worn especially in the 16th century,
>   from Old Spanish toca headdress
> 1: a woman's small hat without a brim made in any of various soft close-fitting shapes
> 2. a tall brimless hat worn by a chef – called also toque blanche

The chef's hat originated when a royal cook in the employ of King Henry VIII started going bald. Henry found a hair in his soup, had the cook beheaded, and ordered the next chef to start wearing a hat. (The cook was only too happy to comply.) Actually, there are a couple of different theories about the origin of the chef's hat, or toque, and there is probably some truth in both.

Some say the toque can be traced back to the seventh century A.D., when chefs were considered learned men. (Remember that "epicurean" derives from the name of Greek philosopher, Epicurus.) Learned men didn't always get the respect they deserved, though, and were often persecuted; at such times, they frequently took refuge in the local church, where they donned the same costumes that the local clergy were wearing, hats and all, as a disguise. Eventually, not wanting to incur the wrath of God any more than the wrath of the local savages, they started wearing white hats instead of the black hats worn by Greek Orthodox priests, and the toque was born.

The other most prominent story about the history of the toque is that it comes to us from the ancient Assyrians. Since one of the more common ways to do in His Royal Highness back then was to poison his food, chefs were chosen carefully and treated very well, often even holding rank in the king's court. Legend has it that the chef's high position entitled him to wear a "crown" of sorts, in the same shape as the king's, though made out of cloth and without all those bothersome jewels. The crown-shaped ribs of the royal headdress became the pleats of the toque, originally sewn, and later stiffened with starch.

Speaking of pleats, the most widely circulated legend about the toque appears to be one concerning the number of pleats. From "A Pageant of Hats, Ancient and Modern," by Ruch Edwards Kilgour, copyright 1958: It was regarded as natural that any chef worthy of the name could cook an egg at least one hundred ways. The most renowned chefs often boasted that they could serve their royal masters a different egg dish every day in the year, some of them so cleverly prepared, that aside from being highly palatable they had flavors as widely different as completely diverse kinds of foods. Today, noted chefs are seldom called upon to prove their prowess in this manner. Nevertheless, they still wear one hundred pleats on their hat, the old-time symbol of their skill in the egg department.

The toque has changed many times over the years, but most stories about its origins are variations on one of the two above. Since the most dramatic changes in style and shape are attributable to the French, I'd be remiss if I didn't include something from a snobbish Frenchman regarding the decline of toquish excellence. Roger Fessaguet, a previous co-owner of La Caravelle (which, I believe, is in New York), laments, "American chefs don't wear a toque. Could you think of a policeman without a hat? That is part of the full uniform. I still have 12 uniforms. In the old days, I used to send my toques back to France aboard French Line ships, to Havre, where they were washed, ironed and starched by women who knew exactly what to do."

I'm thinking that perhaps the legendary Dining Room chefs forgo wearing a toque because they are confident enough of their culinary talents that they don't require a one-hundred pleat headpiece as a symbol of their skill in the egg, or any other, kitchen department. Roger Fessaguet would, in my book, do well to mimic them…as could a few Christians I know. It's the inner person, the heart, not the showy stuff, the Lord looks on.

Ponderable

There's a world of difference between being rooted in the past, but not buried there.

MENU

One Sabbath when Jesus went to dine at the house of a ruler who belonged to the Pharisees, they were watching Him.

(Luke 14:1)

Prayer: O God, come to our assistance; hasten to help us; receive our prayer as incense, our uplifted hands as a sacrifice. Amen.

What did the Pharisee serve Jesus? A lentil soup? Cucumber salad with oregano and thyme? Quail on a bed of saffron rice and green peas as the entrée, or curried lamb? Dessert of strawberries, almonds, and raisins? I bet it was the best menu his cook could muster.

How would you entertain Jesus for dinner? I can't imagine you would count the cost. Would you invite others? Who? Please don't get bogged down, at least right now, with questions about Luke 14:1 like, I thought Jews of Jesus' day didn't do work on the Sabbath, and cooking is work!...Jesus wasn't particularly fond of the Pharisees! What's the deal dining with one?...Who are "they," and what are they "watching" Jesus for? Rather, center on the menu you would prepare for your meal with the Lord; how the table would be set and who gets to sit closest to the Master. Do you ask Him to offer the table grace? (Who wants their prayer critiqued by the Messiah?!) Has one of your dinner guests been prompted to ask the first question or offer the initial observation, to assure there's no awkward silence as all gather at the table?

He's at the door! Ready or not, here we go!

The Resurrected One is, you know, at the door:

Behold, I stand at the door and knock; if any one hears my voice and opens the door, I will come in to him and eat with him and he with me. (Revelation 3:20)

And He has planned the menu:

I am the Bread of Life; whoever comes to Me shall not hunger and he who believes in Me shall never thirst. (John 6:35)

Ponderable   "Kissin' wears out...cookin' don't." (Traditional Pennsylvania Dutch saying)

Soup

Roasted Tomatoes with Shrimp and Feta

5 large tomatoes, cut into eighths
3 tbsp. olive oil
2 tbsp. minced garlic
3/4 tsp. kosher salt
3/4 tsp. ground black pepper
1-1/2 pounds medium shrimp, peeled and deveined
1/2 cup chopped fresh parsley
2 tbsp. lemon juice
1 cup feta, crumbled

Preheat oven to 450°F. Place tomatoes in a large baking dish. Spoon olive oil and garlic over tomatoes. Sprinkle with salt and pepper and toss. Place on top rack of oven and roast for 20 minutes. Remove dish from oven and stir in shrimp, parsley, lemon juice. Sprinkle with feta. Place back in the oven for another 10 to 15 minutes or until shrimp are cooked. Serve warm with crusty bread or over jasmine rice.

(Bob Williams)

Appetizer

Cuban

1 tbsp. Dijon mustard
8 oz. loaf French bread, cut in half horizontally
8 thin slices of Swiss cheese
6 oz. deli ham
8 sliced dill pickles

Spread mustard evenly over cut sides of bread. Arrange half of cheese and half of ham on bottom half of loaf; top with pickle slices. Repeat layer with remaining cheese and ham, cover with top half of loaf. Cut into quarters.

Heat a large skillet coated with cooking spray over medium high heat. Add sandwiches, press with heavy skillet. Cook 2 minutes on each side.

Yield: 4 servings   (Ron Meadows)

Entrée

Scallops

10 Large scallops
1/2 of a red bell pepper
1 small white onion, diced
1 clove garlic, diced
4 slices of bacon; chopped
white wine
Pinch of paprika
Salt and pepper to taste

Cook bacon until crisp; remove and add onion, peppers, and garlic to the bacon grease; cook for 5 minutes or until onion is opaque. Add wine, bacon, paprika, salt, and pepper and steam, covered, for 5 more minutes. Season scallops with salt and paprika and sear completely on one side in a very hot skillet; flip and sear second side slightly. Deglaze pan with white wine and pour ingredients on top of scallops. Finish in a preheated oven, uncovered, at 500°F for 7 minutes.

(Jamie Nading)

THIRST

Blessed are those who hunger and thirst for righteousness, for they shall be satisfied. (Matthew 5:6)

Prayer: *Once I was lost, but now I am found. Thank You, Jesus, the Light of the world. Amen.*

The Hubbard Peanut Company, Sedley, Virginia, begins one of their written ads,

Around our little crossroads town in Southampton County,
people are truly passionate about peanuts.

Perhaps a plausible substitute for "thirst" is "passionate"…blessed, happy, debonair are those who have a passion for the priorities of God's Kingdom rule. Passionately thirsting and hungering after attitudes and actions that honor the cause of the Christ means avoiding the damning judgment,

I know your works; you are neither hot (passionate) or cold. Would that you were cold
or hot (thirsty)! So, because you are lukewarm, I will spew you out of my mouth (more
literally: you make me so sick to my stomach that I vomit). (Revelation 3:15-16)

Examples of physical thirst fail to approach Jesus' call to thirst after God's righteousness, but what else do we have as illustrations? So…the time I was so thirsty for water that I was passionate about finding it.

For months, while living near Jacksonville, Florida, I had developed a healthy walking program. Most days I walked about forty-five minutes, at a good pace, in and around our home in St. Johns County. One August Saturday morning, feeling friskier than usual, I extended my walk with a new route, through woods adjacent to the golf course. The path was clearly visible. I assumed it lead in and then out of the woods. It did not. Soon I was lost. Very lost.

Weeks earlier a lightening strike had ignited a fire in a portion of the woods. Some downed tree limbs still seeped smoke. An eerie sense soon dominated me: no path; no longer a sense of direction (returning myself to the point of entry wasn't possible); burned-out woods; occasional swamp-like terrain; deafening silence (singing out loud, off key, of course, did little to arrest my anxiety); then rain and lightening; a snake, a fox , a crow startled me. Sweating profusely by the second hour, the need for drinking water became urgent. Anxiety approached near panic. What if I had a heart attack? No one would find me out here. Dorothy and our daughters would never know what happened to their husband/dad. Sure I prayed, and pushed on, very, very tired, but fearful that if I stopped to rest I might not get back up, now in a cold sweat. Water, please!

About the fourth hour I was sure I heard the sound of tires on a paved road. Thank you Jesus! It must have taken a half-hour to follow the sound while I pushed my way through the underbrush, muddy and wet, to the berm. But which way, left or right? I had no idea what road it was. I guessed left and stumbled on. I discovered later I was about six miles from home. A black SUV passed me, hit the brakes and backed up. "Dudley, is that you?!" Chris Batchlor called. "Yeah. Boy am I glad to see you! I need a ride home." I hesitate only briefly to put my exhausted body, clothed in wet and muddy T-shirt, shorts and sneakers, in his clean vehicle. And there it was, in the cup holder, already open but two-thirds full: a bottle of Dasani water. I didn't even ask Chris' permission.

Wouldn't Jesus be happy with me if I desired to serve Him as passionately as I wanted that thirst-quenching water?

Ponderable

For 93 percent of all trips outside the home, for whatever distance or whatever purpose, Americans now get in a car. On average the total walking of an American these days – that's walking of all types: from car to office, from office to car, around the supermarket and shopping malls – adds up to 1.4 miles a week, barely 350 yards a day. That's ridiculous. (Bill Bryson, A Walk in the Woods, Rediscovering America on the Appalachian Trail, 1998)

PREPARED

Be prepared to give an account of the hope that is in you… (I Peter 3:15)

Prayer: *Great is Thy faithfulness, great is Thy faithfulness, morning by morning new mercies I see; all I have needed Thy hand hath provided; great is Thy faithfulness, Lord, unto me. (Thomas Obediah Chisholm, 1923)*

For golfers there's no place quite like August National Golf Club, Georgia's home to the Masters. No detail of April's tournament is left to chance. Preparation is key: the beautiful course; parking; spectator guide; security; trash removal; name it. There even are employees posted in the large restrooms to hasten the process, pointing you toward the nearest available toilet/urinal! Most stunning for me was how the food is prepared.

The lines are long, yet a mere three minutes is the average it takes to purchase a pimento cheese or egg salad sandwich on white bread (a paltry $1.50 each; chicken breast, $2.50) wrapped in green plastic (In case it accidentally blows away, it will blend in with the grass and appear less like litter until the clean-up crew does their job); drinks already poured (beer: $2, add 50¢ for the souvenir cup); three cashiers at the end of each line; tax included so any change is in quarters only, hurrying along the process. Preparation is everything at the Masters.

The player's preparation is even more extensive. Tiger, Ernie, Phil, Vijay, and their compatriots, day after day nearly year round, spend enormous time and energy preparing on the practice tee, putting green, and in the sand trap, as well as doing conditioning (both physical and mental) exercises. Preparation is everything for the professional golfer.

How have some of us convinced ourselves that we can be professional disciples of Jesus with only casual preparation – without daily Bible study and prayer, without regular attendance at worship, without frequently coming to the Lord's Table, without sharing our faith questions and convictions with others?

Be prepared to give an account of the hope that is in you…. (I Peter 3:15)

Live in a region where hurricane season is a reality, and you are foolish not to know what actions to take in order to be prepared: having a disaster plan and supply kit; an identified safe room in your home; a NOAA weather radio; an evacuation route. Henry County, Georgia, where Dorothy and I reside, has formed a Community Emergency Response Team, people trained by experts in disaster preparedness, first aid, search and rescue, disaster psychology, medical operations and team organization.

The Boy Scouts have had it right for years: Be Prepared. It's dangerous not to be. Even more dangerous for us Christians. A t-shirt I saw in the Bahamas read, "Jesus is coming – look busy." The Bible says, "be prepared," …we must all stand before Christ to be judged…to have our lives laid bare before Him. Each of us will receive what he/she deserves…. (II Corinthians 5:10)

Ponderable

O God, Thou art my God, I seek Thee, my soul thirsts for Thee; my flesh faints for Thee, as in a dry and weary land where no water is. So I have looked upon Thee in the sanctuary, beholding Thy power and glory. Because Thy steadfast love is better than life, my lips will praise Thee. So I will bless Thee as long as I live; I will life up my hands and call on Thy name. My soul is feasted as with marrow and fat, and my mouth praises Thee with joyful lips, when I think of Thee upon my bed, and meditate on Thee in the watches of the night; for Thou hast been my help, and in the shadow of Thy wings I sing for joy. My soul clings to Thee; Thy right hand upholds me. (Psalm 63:1, 3-8 RSV)

SAD

Even in laughter the heart is sad, and the end of joy is grief. (Proverbs 14:13)

Prayer: *If ever the dark comes upon us, O God, let it be Thy darkness. And when we hope for the wrong things, let us wait in that dark until Thou canst make us ready for what Thou hast promised; through Jesus Christ our Lord. Amen. (Paul Scherer, Love Is a Spendthrift, 1961)*

I n over forty years of ordained ministry in the Presbyterian Church (U.S.A.), all the times that I've preached from Luke 24, Jesus' post-resurrection appearance on the road to Emmaus, it wasn't until recently that I noticed the conclusion of verse 17...

And they stood still, looking sad.

It's a description, you likely know, of the two followers of Jesus who have not yet heard the news, the too-good-not-to-be-true news, that the Lord has risen.

Each of us has our sadness list. I hope yours is short. Mine includes the last lunch I prepared for my only sibling, Kathy. Three years younger than I, my sister died in November, 2004, from a cancer that began in her brain. The dying process was awful. Husband Don Ondo, and children Kim and Nick, with their families, provided Kathy – in cooperation with a wonderful hospice ministry – with beautiful care at home during the final months.

Dorothy and I flew to Pittsburgh, Pennsylvania, for a third time to visit. The last trip was to say good-bye. Powerless to do much of anything, I resorted to my ministry in the kitchen. Remembering that as a teenager Kathy was fond of BLT's, a short drive to the market purchased the bacon, lettuce, tomato, bread, and mayonnaise…and an avocado. Taking orders from family and hospice volunteers gathered in the apartment, I announced I had the traditional BLT as well as avocado substituted for tomato. With the slightest of grins, Kathy mumbled an order for a sandwich with avocado. I don't peel one now without thinking of her.

When I joined Kathy and Don's Pastor in conducting her funeral service in Grove City, Pennsylvania, I spoke on these two texts,

In the world you have tribulation, but be of good cheer, I (Jesus) have overcome the world. (John 16:33b)
Sadness endures for the night, but joy comes in the morning. (Psalm 30:5)

I return each month, sad, from my two-hour visit with Michael. State prison, Jackson, Georgia, Inmate #707503, death row; at last count, thirty-one in his cell block. After twenty-two years of robbing banks (convicted of 127 robberies); doing cocaine;

having had two wives, an engagement, several girlfriends and one child – a son killed in a motorcycle accident – Michael shot and killed the driver of a car he hijacked attempting to flee the scene of a burglary. Kansas born; "I've been on my own since I was thirteen"; neither parents nor brother have any contact with him. "Sparky is waiting for me. My only hope is to die a natural death. I'll never get out of prison."

He and a couple other inmates tried once. "We were fourteen hours away from escaping." Part of the punishment is to be always in handcuffs when out of his cell. Michael and I write between visits, though there's not much to say. I send copies of my sermons, a The New Yorker cartoon now and then and outlines of my week's work. He details daily life on death row; includes sketches (quite an artist); tells of the miserable food; thanks me for being a friend; asks what I think about this or that Bible passage. Michael's envelopes are stamped with the notice that prison authorities have read the correspondence before authorizing their mailing.

Occasionally I include a cashier's check to be deposited in his account. Michael spends it on art supplies and snacks at the prison "store." He says the highlight of his week is being able to buy cheese crackers and candy, etc. Sad. But I'm able to bring a hint of light into Michael's darkness…and he into mine. While it is "more blessed to give than to receive" (Acts 20:35), I trust you've discovered that regularly it is in the giving that we receive.

Ponderable

"When the devil discovers that he cannot rob us of eternity,
then he turns to the insidious task of helping us waste time."
(St. Francis of Assisi)

HEALED

When Jesus arrived at Peter's house, Peter's mother-in-law was in bed with a high fever. But when Jesus touched her hand, the fever left her; and she got up and prepared a meal for them. (Matthew 8:14-15)

The leader of the local synagogue, Jairus, came pleading to Jesus, asking Him to heal his twelve- year- old daughter....While Jesus paused on His way to Jairus' house to heal a woman with a long- standing hemorrhage, messengers arrived with the news that it was too late – the little girl had died. But Jesus ignored their comments. "Don't be afraid. Just trust me."...Taking the child by her hand, Jesus said to her, "Get up, little girl." And she jumped up and walked around! Her parents just couldn't get over it....Jesus told them to give her something to eat. (Mark 5:21-42, portions)

Prayer: *O God, our help in ages past, our hope for years to come, our shelter from the stormy blast, and our eternal home. (Isaac Watts, 1719)*

The most accurate literal translation of the Greek New Testament at the conclusion of Matthew 8:15 is that Peter's mother-in-law "ministered unto them." I'm satisfied that The Living Bible translation, "prepared a meal for them," is the way she ministered. Who "them" are isn't told to us, either by Matthew's Gospel or Luke's (4:38-39). A reasonable guess is that Peter and his wife were present. Likely a couple of good friends. Maybe a neighbor. Could be that the physician and even the local rabbi also were there (although Peter wasn't in good standing with his "parish church," what with being known as up close and personal with the religious rebel Jesus).

Peter's Mother-in-law, fever gone and suddenly feeling fit, does what many a lovable mother-in-law (like mine, June) does to say thanks – prepares one of her signature meals. How many times have you joined me in thinking a thank you note simply won't be sufficient, "so please be my guest for dinner as a gesture of my deep appreciation." Say it with flowers is a nice concept. Say it with food appeals more to me. Apparently it did to Rocky's mother-in-law as well.

But how to get a grip on Mark 5?! A seventh grader miraculously raised from the dead by the Giver of Life, and His first instruction is, "Give her something to eat." Will you and I be resurrected hungry?! Will there be a terrific meal awaiting us when we enter heaven, prepared by legendary chefs (maybe James Beard or Julia Child) who have gone on before?! This much seems clear to me: Peter's mother-in-law, as well as Jairus and child, believe as I do – that planning, preparing, and serving food is a splendid way to rejoice.

Ponderable

Six Rules for Eating Wisely

- Don't eat anything your great-great-great-grandmother wouldn't recognize as food (eat food, not food products).

- Avoid foods containing high-fructose corn syrup (highly processed foods).

- Spend more, eat less. (Higher quality food is more nutritious).

- Pay no heed to nutritional health claims on packages (fresh produce, that makes no such claims, is the healthiest).

- Shop at the farmer's market (foods in season, at their peak of nutritional value and flavor).

- How you eat is as important as what you eat (moderate proportions, no seconds or snacks between meals, eating with pleasure).

(Michael Pollan, Time, June 12, 2006)

GRETNA

What does it profit if people say, "I have faith," but they don't have works (action)? If a brother or sister is ill-clad and in lack of daily food, and you say to them, "Go in peace, be warmed and filled," without giving them the material things they need, what does it profit? So faith by itself, if it has no works, is dead. (James 2:14-17)

Morning Prayer: *Lord, our Father in heaven, eternal and all-powerful God, who has led us safely to the beginning of this day, give us this day Your powerful protection and give us the grace not to fall into sin and not to be subject to any kind of danger. Lead us and direct us Yourself in all our actions so that we can always do that which is right in Your sight, through Jesus Christ our Savior. Amen. (John Calvin, Protestant Reformer, 1509-1564)*

Three hearty meals a day. Six days. Twenty-two mouths. Big Jack Candy planned the menus. I spent most of each day cooking and cleaning up. Breakfast: scrambled eggs, bacon, ham, sausage, grits, biscuits, pancakes, bagels, juice, coffee, cereal, fruit. Dinner: marinated grilled chicken breast, meatloaf, vegetables, burgers, baked potatoes, ham and spaghetti. Lunch: planned leftovers from the previous night's dinner, delivered on site to the laborers: meatloaf, lunchmeat, chicken and chicken salad sandwiches, lots of water, ice tea and soft drinks, chips, candy bars, cookies, brownies.

Gretna, Louisiana, across one of New Orleans' bridges…a mission work team I organized to make a dent in the relief effort following Hurricane Katrina. Housed in the small First Presbyterian Church, sleeping on air mattresses in crowded Sunday School rooms, making do with two small bathrooms and four crude "outside" showers. A coalition of McDonough, Georgia, Presbyterians and Munising, Michigan, Lutherans spent long days of hard, filthy work dressed in protective gear, including respirators, "gutting" houses drowned by hurricane-induced flood waters.

Early on we began to tell one another the truth: We dreaded getting up in the morning; detested the work; already had sore muscles; couldn't wait to get back at the end of the day; too easily became, because of near exhaustion, irritated with our co-workers…but somehow still glad we were in Gretna because, well, it was what we knew Jesus wanted us to do.

During one of the morning group devotion times, I thought of an account in Mike Yaconelli's 2002 book, Messy Spirituality: God's Annoying Love for Imperfect People:

In his marvelous book, Letters to My Children, Daniel Taylor describes an experience he had in the sixth grade. Periodically the students were taught how to dance. The teacher would line up the boys at the door of the classroom to choose their partners. One girl, Mary, was always chosen last. Because of a childhood illness, one of her arms was drawn up and she had a bad leg. She wasn't pretty, she wasn't smart, and she was…well…fat. The assistant teacher of Dan's class happened to attend his church. One day, she pulled Dan aside and said, "Dan, next time we have dancing, I want you to choose Mary." Dan couldn't believe it. Why would anyone pick Mary when there was Linda, Shelley or even Doreen? Dan's teacher told him it is what Jesus would have done, and deep inside, he knew she was right, which didn't make it any easier. All Dan could hope for was that he would be last in line. That way, he could choose Mary, do the right thing, and no one would be the wiser. "Instead," writes Dan, "I was first in line. The faces of the girls were turned toward me, some smiling. I looked at Mary and saw that she had half-turned her back to me…(She knew no one would pick her first.) Mr. Jenkins said, 'Okay, Dan – choose your partner!' I remember feeling very far away. I heard my voice say, 'I choose Mary.' Never has reluctant virtue been so rewarded. I still see her face undimmed in my memory. She lifted her head, and on her face, reddened with pleasure and surprise and embarrassment all at once, was the most genuine look of delight and even pride that I have ever seen, before or since. It was so pure that I had to look away because I knew I didn't deserve it. Mary came and took my arm, as we had been instructed, and she stood beside me, bad leg and all, just like a princess. Mary is my age now. I never saw her after that year. I don't know what her life's been like or what she's doing. But I'd like to think she has a fond memory of at least one day in sixth grade. I know I do."

Our mission work team likely won't see again any of the four Louisiana families who, with their homes, were blessed by our sweat…our reluctant virtue. But their appreciative, smiling faces remain with us.

Ponderable

Preach the Gospel at all times. If necessary, use words.
(St. Francis of Assisi)

RECEPTIONS

On the third day there was a marriage at Cana in Galilee and the mother of Jesus was there. Jesus also was invited to the marriage, with His disciples. When the wine failed…. (John 2:1-3a)

Prayer: *O God, our Father, we beseech Thee for wisdom and discernment as we face the problems of our day, for grace and strength as we take up our tasks, and for courage and perseverance as we discharge our duties. May we have a vision of world needs, as well as needs that are close at hand, and a confident assurance that Christ and His gospel can meet every need. Use us, our talents, our time, our possessions, in the supplying of these needs, we pray. May we help and encourage one another, each day, in all the phases of Kingdom work that Thy children are carrying forward under the guidance of Thy Holy Spirit. For Jesus' sake. Amen. (Prayers For All Occasions, Stuart R. Oglesby, 1940)*

- **The third day:** Jesus' first day in Galilee is described in John 1:43-51 ("The next day Jesus decided to go to Galilee, and…."). What the Lord did on His second day in Galilee is not recorded.

- **There was a marriage:** William Barclay (The Daily Study Bible commentary) explains the wedding custom of Jesus' earthly days: In Palestine, a wedding was a really notable occasion. It was the Jewish law that the wedding of a virgin should take place on a Wednesday. The wedding festivities lasted for far more than one day. The wedding ceremony itself took place late in the evening, after a feast. Following the ceremony, the young couple was conducted to their new home. By that time it would be dark and they were taken through the village streets with the light of the flaming torches and with a canopy over their heads. They were escorted by as long a road as possible so that many people would have the opportunity to wish them well. But in Palestine a newly married couple did not go away for their honeymoon; they stayed at home; and for a week they kept open house. They wore crowns and dressed in their bridal robes. They were treated like a king and queen and their word was law. In a life where there was much poverty and constant hard work, this week of festivity and joy was one of the supreme occasions in life.

- **At Cana in Galilee:** A village very close to Nazareth.

- **And the mother of Jesus was there:** Joseph likely had already died….Apparently Mary was a guest who had something to do with planning/hosting the reception, because she's concerned that the wine has run out….One Church tradition says that Jesus' mother was a sister of the bridegroom's mother.

- **Jesus also was invited to the marriage, with His disciples:** Notes Arthur John Gossip (The Interpreter's Bible), "There is the fact the Christ was there; that they wanted Him to be there; had no fear that He would be out of His element, or fail to fit in, or make others uncomfortable, as John the Baptist, with his asceticism, would have done. And be sure there was no awkward silence at that part of the table where He sat. For Christ did not hold aloof from innocent human happiness – a fact which many of His followers have forgotten, making His religion a more austere thing than He ever did. St. Teresa disliked gloomy people, and prayed to be delivered from frowning saints; and was herself in spite of her devotion – rather because of her devotion and as a real part of it – a happy-hearted person. 'Sometimes she would speak of the weightiest subjects; at others she would say things for our entertainment; sometimes, again, she would make up verses, and very good ones too,' reports one of her nuns."

- **When the wine failed:** A Jewish feast without wine was unthinkable because Eastern hospitality was a sacred duty, and, said the Rabbis, "Without wine there is no joy." Not wine to produce drunks (for drunkenness in the first century was as disgraceful as it should be considered today), but wine (usually consumed as two parts wine with three parts water) to gladden the heart. I think of the Latin proverb, In Vino Veritas (In wine there is truth).

If you or someone you love falls into the category described by The Interpreter's Bible commentary,

> Christ did not hold aloof from innocent human happiness –
> a fact which many of His followers have forgotten,

you may do well to offer…better yet, sing…a prayer,

> Dance, then, wherever you may be, I am the Lord of the Dance said He.
> And I'll lead you all wherever you may be, and I'll lead you all in the Dance, said He.
> ("I Danced in the Morning," Sydney Carter, 1963)

Ponderable

"Too much sugar, too much fat, too many meals on the run and not enough vegetables or variety. Could it be that Americans' worst eating habits all take root in the high chair and stroller? Consider this: by age two, according to a 2002 survey, 1 in 5 babies is eating candy every day. And the number one vegetable for toddlers isn't pureed peas or carrots: it's French fries. Little wonder America has exploding obesity rates among the very young." (Pamela Paul, Time, June 12, 2006)

REST

"Be still, and know that I am God." (Psalm 46:10)

Prayer: *Dear Lord and Father of mankind, forgive our foolish ways.…O Sabbath rest by Galilee, O calm of hills above, where Jesus knelt to share with Thee the silence of eternity. Amen. (John G. Whittier)*

Let the meat or poultry rest about five minutes before you carve it, the knowledgeable ones say, thus avoiding the loss of too many tasty juices. How about five minutes at the end of the day for a prayer period so we don't lose too many life juices?

- **Review the day.** Identify the places God has been at work in your life and give thanks.

- **Confess.** Note your feelings, actions, and choices which have been contrary to God's will in Christ. Be specific. Acknowledge those and accept God's forgiveness.

- **Commit.** Release yourself to God for the night. Ask the Lord to let you drift into sleep, conscious of God's loving presence.

The last I heard, they closed the Tokyo Zoo for two days a month because the stress of animals having to live day after day in the public eye, with little time to themselves, caused problems. Where is your zoo?

> After Jesus had dismissed the crowds, He went up into the hills, by Himself,
> to pray. When evening came, Jesus was there alone. (Matthew 14:23)

By habit a morning person – an early morning person – I offered to save the custodial team at the Miami Central Presbyterian Church (the year I was their Interim Head of Staff) a trip by saying I would unlock the building at 5 a.m. so it could be used by a small group of Korean Presbyterians. As the Church's guests, they meet from 5-7 a.m., five days a week, to pray. There followed a thirty- minute exercise routine in one of the parking lots, then off to work, etc. Some of our folks referred to them as those crazy Koreans. Hardly. Combining spiritual and physical exercise/discipline makes for healthier Christians. It's no surprise to me that the fastest-growing churches in the Presbytery of Greater Atlanta are Korean congregations.

- How is your diet going?

- Are you a member of the Underslept Society?

- Do you know nutrition is as much a spiritual decision as is prayer?

- Have you laughed recently, especially at yourself?

- James Thurber described Jim Ross, founder of The New Yorker, as "living at the corner of work and worry." You too?

- Are you prepared to act on, "I must ruthlessly eliminate hurry from my life"? A sixth grade son asked his dad, "Why do you always bring work home from the office?" "I can't get it done at work." "Couldn't they put you in a slower group?"

- Divert Daily; a least a few unrushed moments before God

- Withdraw Weekly; a day off, away from the fray

"I come to the Garden alone, while the dew is still on the roses, and the voice I hear, falling on my ear, the Son of God discloses. And He walks with me, and He talks with me, and He tells me I am His own; and the joy we share as we tarry there, none other has ever known." (C. Austin Miles)

Up north, I used to play tennis with a minister friend once a week. When we scheduled our first game he insisted it be on an old court tucked back in the woods. I proposed we use the newer courts at the high school. He refused, saying, "Members of my congregation might see us on those courts playing week after week, and be upset that I'm not working. I'd rather go where no one is likely to see us and discover I take an hour-and-a-half off a week." With a divine spark of inspiration I said, "Listen, you're committing adultery." "What?!" "Sure you are. You're marrying the Church, devoting every bit of your life to Her, and the Church already is married to Christ – His Bride…so you're committing adultery!" I quoted Ecclesiastes 3,

> For everything there is a season, a time for every matter under heaven…
> and God has made everything beautiful, in its time…

including intentional time for work and worship, prayer and play, family and fun, reading and recreating.

Slow dancing in life's fast lane yields healthier believers.

> Take time to be holy, speak oft with the Lord; abide in Him always,
> and feed on His Word. Make friends of God's children; help those who
> are weak; forgetting in nothing His blessing to seek. (W. D. Longstaff)

Ponderable

Somewhere in Charles Swindoll's volumes of books, he turns his Christian creativity loose like this,
Pussy cat, pussy cat, where have you been? I've been to London to look at the Queen.
Pussy cat, pussy cat, what did you there? I frightened a little mouse under her chair.

Dr. Swindoll then comments,

"Stupid cat! She had the chance of lifetime. All of London stretched out before her.
Westminster Abbey, the British Museum, Ten Downing Street, Trafalgar Square,
the House of Parliament, St. Paul's Cathedral. She could have snuck in to hear
the London Philharmonic or scrambled up an old wooden lamp post to watch
the changing of the guard. Not this cat. She had work to do…mice to chase.
She was a mouseaholic who couldn't stop the same old grind. All that mattered
was finding a mouse to frighten under the Queen's chair. Can you imagine the
scene as her husband met her plane back in Los Angeles? "Hi, Fluff! How was
London? Tell me all about it." "Well, Tom, it all started when I saw this mouse.""

Salad

Fall Salad With Pecans

1 head red leaf lettuce – bite size pieces
1 head bib lettuce – bite size pieces
2 red delicious apples – cut into thin wedges
3/4 cup crumbled blue cheese
3/4 cup chopped pecans

Dressing: 1/2 cup vegetable oil
1/4 cup cider vinegar
2 T. shallots, minced
1 T. maple syrup
Put ingredients in a jar with lid and shake.

Glazed Pecans: 1/4 cup butter
1/4 cup corn syrup
2 T. water
salt
1/2 pound pecans

Preheat oven to 250°F. Line baking sheet with foil. Combine butter, corn syrup, water, and salt in saucepan; bring to a boil. Add pecans; stir to coat nuts. Spread nuts evenly on baking sheet. Bake 1 hour, stirring every 10 minutes.

Add apples, pecans, and blue cheese to lettuce; then add dressing. Serves 10.

(Kim North)

Appetizer

Pan Con Tomate

1 loaf French bread
olive oil and salt, to taste
4 tomatoes, roasted
2 Tbsp. red wine vinegar
2 Tbsp. olive oil
1 clove garlic, chopped
salt to taste

Slice bread 1/4-inch thick and place on sheet pan. Drizzle with olive oil and salt; bake in a preheated oven at 350° F for 10-12 minutes. Let cool. Use food processor to crush tomatoes; add olive oil, garlic, vinegar, and salt. Smooth paste onto bread. Garnish with parsley, if desired, and more olive oil.

(Lucinda Wirt)

Soup

Black Bean

1 medium onion, chopped
4 cloves garlic, minced
1 tablespoon ground cumin
1/2-1 teaspoon crushed red pepper flakes
2 tablespoons vegetable oil
3 (16 oz.) cans black beans, undrained
2 cups chicken broth
3 cups mild or medium thick salsa
2 tablespoons lime juice
1/2 cup plain yogurt

Using a 3-or 4-quart saucepan, sauté the onions and garlic with the seasonings in the oil. Stir in the next three ingredients and heat through. Remove from heat and stir in lime juice and yogurt.

Yields: 10 servings

(Betty Meadows)

TREATS

I have learned, in whatever circumstance, to be content…. (Philippians 4:11)

Prayer: *Almighty and everlasting God, who in the Paschal mystery hast established the new covenant of reconciliation: grant that all who have been reborn into the fellowship of Christ's Body may show forth in their lives what they profess by their faith; through the same Jesus Christ our Lord, who liveth and reigneth with Thee and the Holy Spirit, one God, for ever and ever. Amen. ("Collect for the Second Sunday of Easter", The Episcopal 1979 Book of Common Prayer)*

He lives in a six by 12-foot room (cell #29) on Death Row, at the Georgia Department of Corrections in Jackson, Georgia. We correspond by letter, an occasional collect phone call, and my monthly two- hour visits. Michael Nance, UNO #707503, shot and killed a man while hijacking a car following one of his numerous bank robberies. Meals at G.D.C.P. are not gourmet. It's a real treat for Michael to buy from the prison "store" salt and pepper and especially picante sauce to spice up the bland food,. Born into a Jehovah's Witness family in Kansas, with a Spanish father and Cherokee Indian mother, he delights in a taste of the old days on the outside – symbolized by a jar of picante sauce.

Ask my friends Skip and Lyn Lampe what their favorite food treat is and you'll hear…lobster. He dives for them in the Florida Keys. She prepares them in butter and wrapped lettuce leaves (keeps them moist) on the grill or under the broiler. Perfect! Though when Skippy and I took a leisurely week's car trip years ago from our homes near Jacksonville, Florida, to Canton, Ohio's Pro Football Hall of Fame, driving the back roads, stopping whenever and wherever our whims took us, the only constant was his insistence that each day begin with breakfast at a Hardee's. Hardly my idea of a treat, (make it lobster for me, breakfast too) but, to each his own.

A couple was seated at the table next to Dorothy and me at Montreal's Bonaparte Restaurant. The fairer of the two inquired of the waiter, after examining the menu, "Is the she-crab soup good?" "Madam," he replied with a straight face, "you will remember it for the rest of your life." A lovely exaggeration! I already had enjoyed my cup. Very good it was, but for the rest of your life?! When asked by the waiter as he removed her empty cup, "I hope you enjoyed the soup?," she smiled and replied, "It was a real treat."

The treat at Brad and Gloria Christie's home in Due West, South Carolina, for their three sons (the youngest, Luke, the 2006 national poster child for Jerry Lewis' muscular dystrophy campaign) is candy. Serious about following Jesus, this delightful and talented family keeps a jar of candy on top of the refrigerator. It's passed out not as a reward for being good or getting an "A" or any such accomplishment. Instead, mom or dad takes the jar down randomly and offers a piece to their sons. They call it "grace candy."

Picante sauce…lobster…Hardee's 99¢ special…she-crab soup…candy: treats, expensive and inexpensive. This is one of those times when it's all relative. One secret to a satisfying walk with Christ is to learn to be content in whatever our circumstance.

Ponderable

O Lord, Thou art our Father; we are the clay and Thou art the Potter.
We are the works of Thy hand. (Jeremiah 64:8)

We have this treasure (the Gospel) in ordinary clay pots (us), to show
that the transforming power belongs to God, not to us. (II Corinthians 4:7)

ADJUSTMENT

"I have learned, in whatever circumstance, to be content...." (Philippians 4:11)

Prayer: *Grant, O God, deep peace of the running waves, deep peace of the flowing air, deep peace of the quiet earth, deep peace of the shining stars, deep peace of the Son of peace. Amen. (A Celtic Prayer)*

When I was doing my penance for the sin of divorce by working as a salesman (Bob, Harry and Jack of the James Austin Company graciously created the position for me), I made a monthly overnight trip to Huntington, West Virginia. At the hotel where I lodged, the bar advertised their Happy Hour as Attitude Adjustment. Most of our attitudes need an adjustment, at least occasionally, but alcohol isn't (or shouldn't be) required.

When friend Jack North, a marvelous motivational speaker, represents State Farm Insurance on the circuit (among his many other responsibilities as one of only three Senior Executive Vice-Presidents with the Company), a frequent theme is a healthier version of attitude adjustment. Jack's presentations often detail his usual parting statement to folks: "Make it a good day." Not, mind you, "Have a good day." Have likely depends on the circumstances; make is a result of one's attitude, response, toward daily circumstances.

Brother Lawrence (The Practice of the Presence of God, 1895) didn't much care for the circumstances of those times when assigned to work as a cook in the monastery's kitchen. But he adjusted his attitude, teaching himself to feel very close to God even in that setting. In fact, he led himself to the point of believing that in the kitchen he often felt closer to God than even when kneeling at the altar in the presence of the Blessed Sacrament!

E. Allison Peers in Mother of Carmel (1945) writes of St. Teresa,

> She was very fond of engaging in the lowliest and humblest duties; and her companions assure me that, when it is her week to do the cooking, they never lacked for anything. And how could they? For, said Teresa... "The Lord walks among the pots and pans, just as much as in the Garden of Eden, and He will help you in the tasks of inward life and of the outward life too."

Life is much about attitude...a lesson well learned from the table and kitchen.

Ponderable

"The privilege of prayer to me is one of the most cherished possessions, because faith and experience alike convince me that God sees and answers, and His answers I never venture to criticize. It is only my part to ask. It is entirely His to give or withhold, as He knows best. If it were otherwise, I would not dare to pray at all. In the quiet of home, in the heat of life and strife, in the face of death, the privilege of speech with God is inestimable. I value it more because it calls for nothing that the wayfaring man, though a fool, cannot give – that is, the simplest expression to his simplest desire. When I can neither see, nor hear, nor speak, still I can pray so that God can hear. When I finally pass through the valley of the shadow of death, I expect to pass through it in conversation with Him." (Sir Wilfred Grenfell)

CONTROVERSY

On the Sabbath day, as Jesus and His disciples were walking through the fields, the disciples were breaking off wheat and eating the grain.   (Mark 2:23-28)
(I'm thinking of our Lord's petition in His model prayer: Give us this day our daily bread…
including on the Sabbath day)

Prayer: *Strengthen and direct me, Lord of the Sabbath, to insist on sanctifying the preparing and enjoying of food, primarily for ones for about whom I have a special affection, and especially on the Sabbath. Amen.*

Just before these verses which conclude chapter two of St. Mark's remembrances of Jesus' teachings, the Gospel writer noted the controversy over fasting. Now comes the report of how the Lord responded to the Sabbath controversy:

> The Sabbath was made to benefit people, and not people
> to benefit the Sabbath. And as the Messiah, I have authority
> to decide what people can do on the Sabbath.

Bold indeed! Little wonder God's Son provokes the wrath of the established religious traditionalists. Jesus is not done yet. Mark opens chapter three (verses 1-6) by reporting how Jesus handled the controversy over His Sabbath healing of the man with a deformed hand, beginning with the Christ's taunting questions to His opponents,

> Is it all right to do kind deeds (like healing) on Sabbath days? Or is this a day
> for doing harm? Is the Sabbath a day to save lives or destroy them?

The controversy in Mark 2:23-28 for some of us today is that Jesus doesn't get it right when He makes reference to I Samuel 21:1-6! Using King David as a precedent for His disciple's Sabbath grain harvesting/working and eating (When David and his men were hungry they went to the Temple and devoured the special bread, called "show", which was only for the priests to eat), Mark has Jesus say it occurred when Abiathar was the high priest (Mark 2:26). Fact is, it was Ahimelech, Abiathar's father, who was high priest (I Samuel 21:1). No big deal, you say? Such a minor mistake…don't let it get in the way of the important Truth Jesus is arguing for.

But it's not a small matter if you're in the mold of Bart D. Ehrman…born and raised in Lawrence, Kansas…involved with his family in the local Episcopal Church as a child…had a genuine "born again" experience as a high school sophomore through the influence of Campus Life Youth for Christ…enrolled at Moody Bible Institute in 1973, agreeing with their conviction that the Bible is the inerrant Word of God (contains no mistakes because it is verbally inspired by God)…felt called to become a

Biblical scholar representing the evangelical (conservative) view of scripture…so continued his education at Wheaton College (the alma mater of Billy Graham)…was encouraged by a Wheaton professor to pursue studies in textual criticism of the New Testament with the world's leading expert in the field, Bruce M. Metzger, at Princeton Theological Seminary.

In Bart's second semester at Princeton, he took a course on the Gospel of Mark with a much revered and pious professor, Cullen Story (as I did in 1968). The final paper was to be an examination of a passage in Mark. Ehrman selected Mark 2:23-28, discovering in his research Jesus' error about Ahimelech/Abaiathar as the high priest. Hear his response, from Bart's 2005 book, Misquoting Jesus: The Story Behind Who Changed the Bible and Why,

> In my paper for Professor Story, I developed a complicated argument that even though Mark indicates this happened "when Abiathar was high priest," it doesn't really mean that, rather that the event took place in the part of the scriptural text that has Abiathar as one of the main characters. My argument was based on the meaning of the Greek words involved and was a bit convoluted. I was pretty sure Professor Story would appreciate the argument, since I knew him as a good Christian scholar who obviously (like me) would never think there could be anything like a genuine error in the Bible. But at the end of my paper (I got a good grade) he made a simple one-line comment that for some reason went straight through me. He wrote, "Maybe Mark just made a mistake." I started thinking about it…realized that I had to do some pretty fancy exegetical (interpreting of the Greek words) to get around the problem, and that my solution was in fact a bit of a stretch. I finally concluded, "Maybe Mark DID make a mistake." Once I made that admission, the floodgates got opened.

One result of the personal controversy over interpreting Mark 2 that "opened the floodgates" for Bart Ehrman is that some of us, myself in that number, have been aided immensely by his Biblical scholarship. For the record: at this writing he chairs the Department of Religious Studies at the University of North Carolina at Chapel Hill, and is recognized as an authority on the history of the New Testament, the early Church, and the life of Jesus…and remains a devout Christian.

When I was young in ordained ministry as a parish Pastor and budding theologian, I feared controversy of any kind. Having grown up some now, I am persuaded that honest questions about the life of the Church and about the Bible's Truth can be, even if rough waters to navigate, productive to the God Movement. As Fred Buechner says about honest doubt, so I believe about controversy, It can be the ants in the pants of faith – helping to keep it alive and moving.

Ponderable

> "I believe Lord, help Thou my unbelief." (Mark 9:24)

WELCOME

Welcome one another, as Christ has welcomed you, for the glory of God. (Romans 15:7)
Jesus said, "I was a stranger and you welcomed Me...." (Matthew 25:31ff)

**Morning
Prayer:**
I bind unto myself today the strong name of the Trinity, by invocation of the same: the Three in one and one in Three. I bind this day to me forever by power of faith, Christ's incarnation; His baptism in the Jordan River; His death on the cross for my salvation. Praise to the Lord of my salvation. Salvation is of Christ the Lord. (St. Patrick's Breastplate)

It was the restroom closest to the Church offices, across the hall from the smallest of Broadmoor Presbyterian Church's kitchens and fellowship halls. I did well to time my trips during weekday mornings so as to avoid the crowd of youngsters who would be released for bathroom breaks in small groups from the Baton Rouge Church's preschool program. It would not be good to have a female teacher standing halfway into the restroom, door propped open, to monitor the little boys' behavior while I was involved in ministerial relief!

But one morning I was caught. In they poured. Standing at a urinal, the child beside me looked up in puzzlement and then declared, "Hey mister, you're too big to pee in here." As far as he was concerned, it was his bathroom and big guys weren't welcome.

April 23, 2006, the first Lord's Day after Easter, and I had a Sunday "off"...off from the usual responsibility and privilege of leading worship and preaching. A change-of-pace Service was appealing: Christ Church (Episcopal) on Frederica Road, St. Simons Island, Georgia.; eight a.m. – the first of three, and the most informal (but still a wonderfully "high church" liturgical experience); forward to the kneeler to receive Holy Communion. I very much appreciated the bulletin announcement:

> All baptized Christians who receive Communion in their home churches are invited
> to receive the Sacrament of the Eucharist. Children who have not yet received
> Communion instruction, and others who wish a blessing, may come to the altar rail
> with their arms crossed. It is appropriate to either stand or kneel at the rail.

A brief and helpful homily was offered by the new rector (his first Lord's Day at Christ's Church); sixty or so worshippers in the small, historic Sanctuary surrounded by an old and well-preserved cemetery; no music of any sort at this Service; very quiet and worshipful before and during the forty minutes. (If folks talked, it was in the lowest of whispers...most greetings consisted of a smile and nod of the head.)

I sat alone, wishing I had a 1928 Book of Common Prayer so I could participate more actively in the Order of Worship. I was a stranger in that lovely all-wood and beamed Sanctuary. No one smiled at me or greeted me with a nod of the head, not even on the way to the parking area, except the usher who shook my hand and handed me a bulletin with a "good morning" as I entered. Perhaps it would have been different at the 9:30 or 11:15 a.m. service. It was their church, it felt like to me – a bit like the lad's bathroom. I was glad to be present and was helped spiritually by the worship experience, but….

Earlier that week, friend Lewis Robinson had treated me to a splendid meal at Delaney's Bistro (a sweet red chili-glazed smoked duck breast appetizer, veal chop with shitake mushrooms and brown sauce, etc.). Mark, the waiter, mentioned that on Monday they were offering a six-course wine dinner…matching Scott Harvey wines with some of Tom Delaney's food specialties: $75. I signed up, then arrived at 6:30 p.m. for appetizers, with the chef's tasting menu beginning to be served at 7:15. (My favorite was the sautéed diver scallops with curry, paired with a 2003 Zinfandel.) I was a stranger once again. The fifty-some diners, who knew others in the room, mingled as I stood alone near my table set for one. Until Kate, David, and mother/mother-in-law, Ann, moved to their assigned table for four next to me. Immediately Kate asked, "Are you alone? Would you join us?" No longer a stranger. A lovely gift. And that simple…especially for Christians who accept the Truth of this chapter's Biblical verses.

Enjoyable conversation around the table followed: about food, cooking techniques, wine, theology, my book, church music, our families, places we have lived. Ann is in real estate…David owns a motorcycle store in West Palm Beach (and is something of a food and wine connoisseur), and Kate is Director of Music at St. William Roman Catholic Church. As we concluded the lovely evening at 10 p.m., a second invitation was issued: "Would you be our guest for dinner at our home Friday evening? We'll all cook together. It will be fun. No one ought to eat alone."

Welcome one another, as Christ has welcomed you, for the glory of God.

And so I did, joined by some of their church friends (Maureen, church kitchen coordinator; Dick and Barbara, part-time church secretary; Lois, organist). Incidentally, the best Roman Catholic one-liner of the evening: The Pope has bird flu; got it from a Cardinal.

I brought a couple appetizers (cream cheese and blue cheese with basil pesto; sliced tomatoes on bite sized Italian bread, topped with salt and pepper, chopped onion, fresh basil leaf, red wine vinegar, and extra virgin olive oil) and decent bottles of wine (Chardonnay to accompany the cheese dip and a Pinot Noir with the tomatoes). I watched, learned and assisted David as he worked magic with chicken breasts (pounded thin, browned quickly in butter, then poached in chicken broth, sliced lemons, sage [made crisp by sautéing in butter, without letting the butter brown], etc.) Served with couscous, wilted greens and snow peas on one plate. Very nice. Kate had set an elegant table: linen, china from her amazing collection, crystal, candles. David's creme brulee, with chocolate on the bottom of the ramekin, was perfect.

More perfect: a stranger made to feel at home. Go and do likewise. It glorifies God.

Ponderable

It is an unforgettable scene there in that upper room – the shadows, the stillness, the hushed voices of people speaking very carefully, very intently, because they wanted to get it all said while there was still time and to get it said right. You can only imagine the way it must have haunted them for the rest of their lives as they looked back on how they had actually sat there with Him, eating and drinking and talking; and through 2,000 years of the Church's re-enactment of it in the Eucharist, it has come to haunt us too.

But I think of the Lord's Supper as haunting in another way as well – not just as a kind of shadowy dream of an event long past but also as a kind of foreshadowing of an event not all that far in the future, by which I mean our own last suppers, the last time you and I will sit down with a handful of our own closest friends. It's hard not to believe that somehow or other there's always going to be another time with them, another day, so the chances are we won't know it's the last time, and therefore it won't have the terrible sadness about it that the Last Supper of Jesus must have had. But not knowing is sad in another way because it means that we also won't know how precious this supper is, how precious these friends are whom we will be sitting down with for the last time whether we know it or not. (Frederick Buechner, "Bidding Farewell," Christian Century, April 4, 2006)

Entrée

Hot Garlic Shrimp and Asparagus

8 (1/2-inch thick) slices sourdough bread
2 tbsp. olive oil
1 pound sliced asparagus (1-inch pieces)
2 cloves garlic, minced
1/2 tsp. salt
1/4 tsp. crushed red pepper
1/4 tsp. black pepper
1 – 2 pounds large shrimp, peeled and deveined
1 cup dry white wine
2 tbsp. lemon juice

Preheat oven to 400°F. Place bread slices in a single layer on a baking sheet. Bake for 6 minutes or until toasted. Heat oil in a large skillet over medium heat. Add asparagus, garlic, salt, and peppers; cook for 2 minutes, stirring frequently. Add shrimp; cook for 4 minutes, stirring frequently. Stir in wine and juice; bring to a boil. Remove from heat; serve with bread slices.

(Rachael Knoll)

Soup

Gazpacho

1 lb strawberries
3 oz red peppers
3 oz green peppers
1 clove garlic
2 Tbsp. sherry vinegar
1/2 cup olive oil
salt to taste

Clean strawberries and peppers. Puree everything in blender and strain. Add salt to taste. Chill for 2 hours before serving. Garnish with whole strawberries

(Stephen Ingram)

Entrée

Dijon Chops

4 T. Dijon mustard
1/4 t. pepper
salt
4 T. brown sugar
2 T. soy sauce
2 T. olive oil
1/2 head garlic, minced
1/3 cup lemon juice
1/4 cup butter
1 T. Worcestershire
1 T. catsup
dash rosemary
4 thick cut pork chops

In saucepan combine and heat all ingredients except chops. Place chops in a greased 9x13 pan. Pour sauce over chops and bake at 400° F for 20-30 minutes. Remove chops and grill for 10-15 minutes to brown, basting often. Spoon sauce over chops when serving.

(Charlie Landreth)

PLEDGE

Jesus said, "Everyone who acknowledges Me before others, I will acknowledge before the angels of God." (Luke 12:8)

Prayer: *I wait before You, O God: the Creator of the world, the Most High God, the Transcendent One, the Alpha and the Omega, the Beginning and the End, the Source of all Holiness. Speak Lord, Your servant awaits. Amen.*

I was almost certain I heard the voices of Confederate soldiers in the next room. Seated at a long table with twenty others in a restored antebellum home north of Baton Rouge, Louisiana, dining on traditional Southern fare (featuring fried chicken), the atmosphere was conducive to remembering "plantation days." Slave quarters remain on the property. The kitchen still is separated from the house (in the event of fire). Drinks had been served on the wrap-around porch – veranda, they called it. They were a Presbyterian medical doctor and his spouse who had bought the house and acreage from an old Southern family who no longer could afford to maintain it.

I was thrilled to be included on the guest list of those who would arrive on Friday night, be wined and dined, sleep over, and then be treated to a full Saturday morning breakfast of cheese grits, biscuits and gravy (prepared with coffee), smoked bacon, poached eggs on toast from homemade bread, et. al. This would be followed by assisting with the annual round-up of the Texas longhorns housed on the farm. The vet examined them for pregnancy (females, of course) and width of horns (males: Charlie was the winner, measuring fifty-two inches from horn to horn). Annual shots were administered to the animals. My assignment, not too demanding, was to help guide the animals into the "pen" for their examinations, measurement, and inoculations.

It was a once-in-a-lifetime experience, never to be forgotten: finest food, astonishing atmosphere, superb surroundings. Somewhere along the line, if we are to be sincere in our Christian faith, a once-for-all decision for Jesus is required. Surroundings, atmosphere, and food may or may not be part of our decision making. However, a time comes when we who want to be Christ's people must have a never-to-be-forgotten encounter with the Lord, then stand up and be counted:

Jesus is my Lord and Savior. I trust in Him. I intend to be His disciple,
to obey His word and to show His love. I will be a faithful member of this
congregation, giving of myself in every way. (Vows of Church Membership)

Ponderable

Over rocks and mountains the sheep are scattered all around.
Over hills and valleys, they are everywhere to be found.
But though we bear our burdens now, all afflictions got to end somehow:
from swinging the hammer, pulling the plough.
Why won't you let us be, to live in harmony?
We like to be free like birds in a tree.
Hallelujah time! Yes, you can hear the children singing.
Let them sing; never let them cry.
Hallelujah time! "Hallelujah" singin' in the morning.
("Hallelujah", Bob Marley; Jamaican guitarist, songwriter and performer of reggae music)

TABLE D'HOTE

…nevertheless Father, not my will, but Thine, be done. (Luke 22:42)

Prayer: *On this Communion Sunday, O God, we have things on our plates we wish we didn't. But this morning, at Your Table, make us aware of how it can all be changed by the power of Your presence, through Jesus Christ our Lord. Amen. (Robert Cleveland Holland, Robert Holland at Shadyside, 1985)*

In 1985 I had the honor of serving as the Chaplain for a wonderful group in Pittsburgh, Pennsylvania: The Variety Club, Tent #1. Their mission is to support research for Spina Bifida. The annual banquet was held that year at the Fox Chapel Yacht Club. Seated at the head table to offer the invocation, I chatted with the president, Donald H. Reigel, M.D. Knowing I was a Presbyterian clergyman, Dr. Reigel spoke of his home church, Shadyside Presbyterian, and their Head of Staff, The Reverend Doctor Robert Cleveland Holland. Telling me that seventeen of his minister's sermons had just been published in the book noted above, the physician asked if he might send me a copy. It arrived a few days later with a "sticky note" on which he had written to his secretary,

> Please send to the above (my address at the North Sewickly
> Presbyterian Church, Ellwood City, PA) with a note: "I hope this will
> be as meaningful to you as it has been to me!"

It was, and has been, one sermon in particular: "A La Carte or Table d'Hote?", preached February 27, 1983. In it, Dr. Holland writes the following:

> "A la carte" is the kind of menu where each diner self-indulgently builds the contents
> of a private, personal plate, no matter what anyone else is eating. "A la carte," literally,
> "by the bill, off the list, from the card." Then there is "table d'hote," literally, "the host's
> table" – the host's choice, not yours.

The preacher goes on to say, powerfully and profoundly,

> Sin is selfism – me – I make up the menu the way I like it. "A la carte," not just at the
> table, but in my life. The Christian life, however, is "table d'hote." The Host, THE
> HOST, sets before us what He wants us to have. The problem of sin is this: We

want an "a la carte" life, with ourselves in control. God's way is "table d'hote," what
He wants us to have. A lot of prayer starts off right – "Thy will be done; not my
will, but Thine." Then somehow it changes allegiance: "Lord, You do whatever
I want." We do not get to choose everything on our plates. But far more important, no
matter what comes on our plate, God loves us; He sticks with us all the way to the
end, no matter what. What the Host serves He backs up with Himself.

If that doesn't wean you from the sin of selfism – wanting to get more than you want to give – I'm at a loss to know what might.

Ponderable

A sous chef is a chef in ranking just below an executive chef, the chef de cuisine. The word "sous" is French for "under", related to the prefix "sub" in English. Think Andrew, a sous chef to his brother Simon Peter, who became one of the Lord's executive chefs. (John 1:37-42)

AGNES

Jesus said, "The tax collectors and harlots go into the Kingdom of God before you." (Matthew 21:31, 32)

Prayer: *Open our eyes, Lord, we want to see Jesus; to reach out and touch Him and say that we love Him. Open our ears, Lord, and help us to listen. Open our eyes, Lord, we want to see Jesus. Amen. (Robert Cull)*

He's bald, a Baptist, sweats a lot, is hyperactive when he preaches, and is getting old. Tony Campolo is one of my spiritual heroes, an ideal combination of basic (evangelical, they call it) Christianity combined with a relentless Jesus-inspired commitment to social justice.

My faith was bolstered the morning I joined eight hundred or so people for a breakfast in Jacksonville, Florida, where Dr. Campolo was the speaker. I have no recollection of the food served. I suppose it was the usual watery scrambled eggs, two pieces of undercooked bacon, with a dab of canned fruit and a biscuit that would embarrass a Southern cook. But, oh, do I remember the story about Agnes. You can, and should, read the full account in Tony's book of 1990, *The Kingdom of God is a Party.*

Tony was in Hawaii to speak. Because of jet lag his inner clock was confused, leaving him restless at night. Instead of tossing and turning, he made his way to an all-night diner, which also happened to be a gathering place for the people of the night, particularly those women who walk the street. Minding his own business, he overheard a conversation between two prostitutes. "Y'know," said Agnes, "tomorrow's my birthday." "So what," the other said. Agnes went on, "I never had a birthday party, or a cake." After the women left, Tony talked to the waitress and cook and learned the woman's name. It bothered him that Agnes had never had a birthday party. So he decided to give her one. The more he talked it over with others in the restaurant, the more excited they got. And so the plans were laid to surprise the prostitute on her birthday. They decorated the place, bought a cake with candles, and gathered the folks of the night into the diner at the agreed-upon time to wish her well.

When Agnes walked in off the street, she was totally surprised. "Happy birthday to you!" they sang, and gave her the cake. She just stared at it, tears rolling down her cheeks. Then Agnes asked, "Could I take it home with me? I want to show it to my mom." And she did. The place was quiet. At that moment Tony did something that even surprised him. He heard himself ask the people if they'd pray with him for her. They did, these people of the night. Everyone bowed their head and Tony prayed for Agnes, remembering that Jesus had died for her because God loves her very much.

Afterward the cook came up to Tony and said, "You didn't tell us you were a preacher! What church are you from? I'd be part of that kind of church!"

And Tony said with a smile, "A church that throws surprise birthday parties for whores."

That's my kind of church too.

Ponderable

Bill Buford writes in The New Yorker ("TV Dinners: The Rise of Food Television," October 2, 2006), about Julia Child,

> There had been earlier television cooks – James Beard's "I Love to Cook,"
> Dione Lucas' "To the Queen's Taste" – but they were "experts," something
> Child never seemed to be, mainly because what she knew had been learned
> so recently and late in life. Child's culinary education began after she had
> moved to Paris, at the age of thirty-six, accompanying her husband, Paul Child,
> a State Department official, and found herself attending the Cordon Bleu. She
> ended up mastering the national menu, starting a cooking school, and returning
> to the States with a bulky rough draft that would change the American kitchen.
> She never lost that new cook's sense of discovery.

Some of the most exciting followers of Christ I know have never lost the sense of discovery, the "newness," of who Jesus is…what He promises and what He demands.

GHOST
John 15:26-16:15

Prayer: *Spirit of the living God, fall afresh on me. Spirit of the living God, fall afresh on me. Melt me, mold me, fill me, use me. Spirit of the living God, fall afresh on me. (Daniel Iverson, 1935)*

People magazine (November 7, 2005) reports that a 2005 Gallup survey showed that one in three Americans believe in ghosts (up from one in four in 1990). I wonder what a survey among Christians would reveal about the number who believe in the Holy Ghost?

Over the years the laments I've heard about the Apostles' Creed rank in this order: (1) I don't believe in the "holy catholic church," I'm a Presbyterian for goodness sake! (2) No way did Jesus, the sinless One, "descend into hell." (3) I think it's silly these days to believe in ghosts, Holy or not. Let us pause, please, for a moment…before getting onto the heart of this chapter…to offer enlightenment about this ancient Creed (written in Rome in the second century and directed specifically against the teachings of Marcion, who held that matter was evil, that Jesus was not born, and that the Gospel includes no word of judgment, but only grace):

> **1) catholic**, with a small "c" means universal…not the Roman Catholic Church.

> **2) hell** is separation from God (and salvation is reunion with God); the Sinless One assumed the sin of the world on Calvary's cross, thus being separated from God, due to our, not His, sin, and descended into hell.

> **3) Holy Ghost** is best translated Holy Spirit, the Third Person of the Trinity…God the Father, God the Son, and God the Holy Spirit.

The roles of God's Spirit in our lives are abundant. Some are listed in St. John, chapter sixteen. The core of the Holy Spirit's ministry, however, is to re-present Christ today so that Jesus is as alive on this page of God's history as when He walked in flesh and blood on earth.

> When the Counselor (Holy Spirit) comes,
> Whom I shall send you from the Father, even
> the Spirit of Truth, Who proceeds from the Father,
> He will bear witness to Me (re-present Me). John 15:26

"Thank you, Preacher, for clarifying a bit of the Apostles' Creed, and for outlining the task of the Holy Spirit. But, with all due respect, what does it have to do with the theme of your little book on food and meals?" Try this, from Barbara Brown Taylor's Gospel Medicine (1995):

> Eating is so necessary for life, and so is Jesus. Sharing food is what makes us human.
> Most other species forage alone, so that feeding is a solitary business, but human
> beings seem to love eating together. Even when we are stuck alone with a frozen
> dinner, most of us will open a magazine or turn on the television just for company.
> It is, at any rate, one of the clues to Christ's presence. There is always the chance,
> when we are eating together, that we will discover the risen Lord in our midst.

One ministry of the Holy Spirit: re-presenting the risen Lord to us…sometimes at mealtimes.

Ponderable

Live as a wind chime to any breath of the Spirit.
(Matthew Kelty, O.C.S.O., Gethsemani Homilies)

COMMUNITY

They devoted themselves to the apostles' teaching and fellowship, to the breaking of bread and the prayers. (Acts 2:42)

Prayer: *Grant unto us, we do pray Thee, O Lord, loving hearts that shall always be quick to help and sympathize and slow to criticize or hurt. Bind Thy people together with ties of conscious unity, so that a fellowship of love and a warm human understanding may readily be found in their associations with each other at whatever point of church life they may touch. May we be utterly sincere, entirely devoid of selfishness, and wholly open to the warm inflooding experience of the Holy Spirit. In Jesus' name. Amen. (Stuart R. Oglesby, "Prayers for All Occasions," 1940)*

When Stephen Ingram, Director of Youth Ministry, reviewed with me his first draft of a creative curriculum he wrote (with wife Mary Liz's assistance), for what McDonough Presbyterian Church calls Confirmation II (a six-month offering for ninth graders, preceded by a similar program for those in fifth grade, Confirmation I), it contained all the expected. But I was puzzled by the doses of classical spiritual traditions and prayer practices included: a weekend silence retreat (high school freshmen… silent for forty-eight hours?!), a Protestant form of Roman Catholic rosary beads, journaling, walking a labyrinth, references to Eastern Orthodox icons, the Jesus Prayer (Lord Jesus Christ, Son of the living God, have mercy on me, a sinner), Taize music.

"Help me understand this, Stephen! It's going to be a hard sell to Session's Christian Education Committee!" He responded, "There is, with youth – and I imagine with a lot of adults – a spiritual hunger, a longing for a deeper experience of God, 'something more,' and the Church can help young people along that new path by recapturing some old Christian practices." "O.K., but it sounds so individualistic, so self-centered. You know, 'I come to the Garden alone, while the dew is still on the roses, etc." I agree that's a danger, so my curriculum also is heavy on developing implications from a powerful line by Kris Haig, the Minister who heads our Presbyterians Church's Office of Discipleship and Spirituality,

The spiritual journey is not a solo voyage.

For generations, Christians have labeled it "community", and rightly so, because we recognize and respond to God best from within relationships, within a community of faith. Spiritual Lone Rangers don't please God. We are not created to make it alone. Sartre is wrong when in No Exit he pretends hell is other people.

It seems to me that in joining a church you leave home and home town to join a larger world.
The whole world becomes your new neighborhood and all who dwell therein – black, white, yellow, red,
stuffed and starving, smart and stupid, mighty and lowly, criminal and self-respecting, American or
Russian – all become your sisters and brothers in the new family formed in Jesus. By joining a Church you
declare your individuality in the most radical way in order to affirm community on the widest possible scale.
(William Sloan Coffin, Credo)

"They devoted themselves to the apostles' teaching:" We call it Sunday School; attention to the sermons; Bible study, individually and in groups; continuing Christian education courses; reading classic Christian books; and fellowship: "The spiritual journey is not a solo voyage." The breaking of bread: the ancient practice of communion; the sharing of a common life and a common faith… not only at the Lord's Table but at all meals. It may be that the poorer members of the Christian community found the breaking of bread their chief means of subsistence.

"And the prayers:" "Real prayer does not come by gritting our teeth but by falling in love. God invites us into the living room of His heart, where we can put on old slippers and share freely… into the kitchen of His friendship, where chatter and batter mix in good fun…into the dining room of His strength, where we can feast to our heart's delight…into the study of His wisdom, where we can learn and grow and stretch, and ask all the questions we want…into the workshop of His creativity, where we can be co-laborers with Him, working together to determine the outcomes of events…into the bedroom of His rest, where new peace is found, and where we can be naked and vulnerable and free. The key to this home, this heart of God, is prayer." (Richard Foster, Coming Home)

Fred Craddock, one of the "best in the business" of proclaiming the Gospel in a profoundly simple way writes,

Before I married and served in the little mission in the Appalachians, I moved down to a place on Watts Bar Lake, between Chattanooga and Knoxville, a little village. It was the custom in that church at Easter to have a Baptismal service. My church immerses, and it was held, this Baptismal service, in Watts Bar Lake on Easter evening at sundown. Now out on the sandbar, I, with the candidates for Baptism, moved into the water, and then they moved across to the shore where the little congregation was gathered, singing around a fire and cooking supper. They had constructed little booths for changing clothes with hanging blankets. As the candidates moved from the water, they went in and changed clothes and went to the fire in the center. Finally, last of all, I went over, changed clothes, and went to the fire. Once we were all around the fire, this was the ritual of that tradition. Glenn Hickey, always Glenn, introduced the new people, gave their names, where they lived, and their work. Then the rest of us formed a circle around them, while they stayed warm at the fire. The ritual was that each person in the circle then gave her or his name, and said this, "My name is…, and if you ever need somebody to do washing and ironing…" "My name is…If you ever need anybody to chop wood…" "My name is…If you ever need anybody to babysit…" "My name is…If you ever need anybody to repair your house…" "My name is…If you ever need anybody to sit with the sick…" "My name is…. and if you ever need a car to go to town…" and around the circle. Then we ate, and we had a square dance. And then at a time they knew, I didn't know, Percy Miller, with thumbs in his bibbed overalls, would stand up and say, "Time to go," and everybody left. He lingered behind and, with his big shoe, kicked sand over the dying fire. After my first experience of that, he saw me standing there still, and he looked at me and said, "Craddock, folks don't ever get any closer than this." In that little community, they have a name for that. I've heard it in other communities too. In that community, their name for that is "church." They call that "church."

(Craddock Stories, edited by Mike Graves and Richard F. Ward, 2001)

Ponderable

"Our life is like a sailboat that cannot move by its own power but must rely on the force of the wind over which neither the boat nor the sailor has control. Still, a sailor can shift the position of the boat by adjusting the tiller and sheets so that the sails catch the wind. Though it is sometimes a struggle, we can choose to hold the boat of our life steady into the wind of God's Spirit. Then our efforts are supported and directed by grace. One caution: when we open our sails to that Wind, we need to be prepared to go where the Spirit blows." (Marjorie J. Thompson, Soul Feast: An Introduction to the Christian Spiritual Life)

Recommended Restaurants – Favorite Foods...

United States

Alabama
Auburn: *Amsterdam Café* – fried green tomato sandwich
Birmingham: *Tutwiler Hotel* – salmon filet

Florida
Bonita Springs: *Sanibal* – pork chops... *South Bay Bistro* – chocolate soufflé
Jacksonville: *Mediterranie* – rack of lamb
Key West: *Hemmingway's Bar* – conch fritters
Miami: *Joe's Stone Crab* – key lime pie...*Irish Tavern* – "black and tan"
Naples: *Turtle Club* – salmon salad...*Silver Spoon* – catch of the day
St. Augustine: *LePavilion* – crepes...*Raintree* – creme brulee
Tampa (Ybor City): *Columbia* – Cuban sandwich

Georgia
Atlanta: *Twist* – lobster salad...*Vinocity* – white wine and cheese pairing
The Ritz-Carlton (Buckhead) – chef's tasting menu
Touch of India – ask wait staff to order for you
Manuel's Tavern – fish sandwich...*Capital Grill* – lobster-crab cake
Emeril's – fried oysters... *Alon's* – chocolate croissant
Bacchanalia – anything you can afford!...*Varsity* – fried pie
La Fonda Latina – paella... *Kyma* – calamari... *Lumiere* – osso bucco
Clubhouse – martini... *Seegers* – squab
Americus: *Windsor Hotel* (Grand Dining Room) – corn chowder
Columbus: *Olive Branch Café* – escargot...*Chef Lee's* – Peking chicken
Lake Oconee: *Cuscowilia (waterside)* – asparagus salad
Butcher Block – slaw dawg
McDonough: *Truman's* – duck salad
Plains: *Mom's Kitchen* – collards
St. Simons Island: *Chelsea* – sea scallops
4th of May – smoked salmon bagel
The Cloister at Sea Island – tournedos of beef
Savannah: *Cosentino's Trattoria* - Penne Vodka

Illinois
Bloomington: *Country Club* – stuffed chicken breast
Rosie's – onion soup...*Biaggi's* – fettucini with lobster

Louisiana
Baton Rouge: *Phil's Oyster Bar* – oyster po-boy
New Orleans: *La Boucherie* – shrimp bisque

North Carolina
Cashiers: *Cornucopia* – club sandwich... *The Orchard* – venison
Highlands: *Wolfgang's On Main* – wine list...*Wild Thyme* – crab cake sandwich
Highland's Inn – Caesar salad

New York
Manhattan: *Blue Fin* – yellow tail tuna... *Oh! Raku* – sushi
The View (Marriot Marquis) – appetizer bar... *Tonic* – French fries

Ohio
Cleveland: *Winking Lizard Tavern* – pizza... *Rock Bottom* – beer selections
Columbiana: *Dutch House* – chicken and dumplings

Pennsylvania
Grove City: *Rudy and Sons* – spaghetti and meatballs
Ligonier: *Diamond Café* – soup of the day
Mercer: *Iron Bridge* – veal parmesan
Pittsburgh: *Grand Concourse (Station Square)* – brunch buffet...
Buca Di Beppo – antipasto

South Carolina
Charleston: *Slightly North of Broadway* – shrimp and grits

Texas
San Antonio: *Tea Room at Mini Mansions* – quiche
Boudro's Texas Bistro – angus beef

International

Bahamas
(Abaco Sound, Marsh Harbour): Allen and Peter's fresh-caught tuna, prepared on the grill by Greg

Canada
Le Petit Moulinsart (Old Montreal): Mussels offered twenty-two ways
Bonaparte (Old Montreal): She-crab soup
Fairmont (Le Chateau Frontenac) Quebec: Seafood buffet

Ireland
Rosapenna Golf Club (Downing, County Donegal): Irish breakfast

Jordan
Regency Palace Hotel (Amman): Curried lamb stew

Switzerland
Hotel Metropole (Geneva): Lake perch